Spiritual Healing for Tra... Addiction

Through stories and conversations, Drs. Dolores BigFoot and Allyson Kelley reflect on research, clinical work, faith-based topics, spirituality, and recovery. They invite readers to reflect on what it means to walk on a healing path.

Beginning with a brief history of broken spirits and a broken world, the book then discusses the causes of brokenness, vulnerability to brokenness, and healing as a construct of social justice and advocacy. The following chapters cover current aspects of healing from the lens of mental health and substance use, addiction, trauma, and recovery. As much of the world struggles with some aspect of brokenness and healing, stories of enduring well provide examples from all relations and walks of life about healing. Theories and research presented throughout the text support stories and concepts presented. Stories about families, coping, grief, loss, and boundaries give readers resources and exercises to help them become whole. Special consideration is given to healing practices and rituals from Native American communities and families.

This text is a must-have for mental health practitioners, faith-based organizations, communities, individuals and families, programs, and policymakers interested in healing.

Allyson Kelley, DrPH MPH CHES, is a researcher, professor, author, and individual in recovery. She is the principal of Allyson Kelley & Associates PLLC and teaches at the University of North Carolina Greensboro.

Dolores Subia BigFoot, PhD, is a child psychologist by training who holds the Presidential Professorship within the Center on Child Abuse and Neglect at the University of Oklahoma Health Sciences Center.

Spiritual Healing for Trauma and Addiction

Discussions of Mental Health, Recovery, and Faith

**Allyson Kelley and
Dolores Subia BigFoot**

 Routledge
Taylor & Francis Group

NEW YORK AND LONDON

Cover image: © Getty Images

First published 2024
by Routledge
605 Third Avenue, New York, NY 10158

and by Routledge
4 Park Square, Milton Park, Abingdon, Oxon, OX14 4RN

Routledge is an imprint of the Taylor & Francis Group, an informa business

ISBN: 978-1-032-22755-9 (hbk)
ISBN: 978-1-032-22753-5 (pbk)
ISBN: 978-1-003-27401-8 (ebk)

DOI: 10.4324/9781003274018

Typeset in Baskerville
by MPS Limited, Dehradun

This book is dedicated to everyone we lost, because something was broken that did not get healed.

Contents

Figures

Foreword

Our Annishnaabe relatives speak of Seven Fires; a series of human epochs marked by risk and opportunity. After a long period of suffering, some say we have entered the time of the seventh fire, where The People turn back toward the teachings of the Elders and a choice between two paths emerges, which ultimately determines the fate of humanity. The choice it is said entails an opportunity to walk a path of spirit, healing, and connection while the alternative, perhaps focused on individualism, and a reckless expansion of technology and materialism, leads to our annihilation. Another possibility is a merger of the two paths in the formation of a single great nation founded on respect for one another and all of creation.

Euro-Western healthcare systems have long struggled with constructed dichotomies between mind and body, science and spirit, evidence and practice; a struggle which has contributed to a compartmentalization of the human condition as witnessed in an often-fragmented approach to personal and communal wellness. In this important text, Dr. Dolores (Dee) Subia BigFoot and Dr. Allyson Kelley capture the spirit of the healing path and the possibility of a respectful merger of worldviews aimed at good relationships and wellness in the heart, mind, body, and spirit. By focusing on balance as the process and the goal of a healing agenda, leveraging the power of open dialogue, gathering stories of struggle and recovery, and providing practical examples, an invaluable framework for helping and healing work emerges. The text offers an impressive breadth of clinical and traditional knowledge, diving into complex and challenging subjects such as suicide, self-harm, trauma, substance use, violence, and grief while retaining a perspective that is hopeful, strength-based, and recovery-focused. It also provides rich descriptions of successful programs and their processes, which will be of practical use for helpers. But it is more than a clinical text. The inclusion of healing stories and extensive dialogue between Dee and Allyson make the learning journey personal, with the feeling of being at the kitchen table with a wise grandparent sharing love, wisdom, and a vision of a brighter future.

Spiritual Healing for Trauma and Substance Abuse Recovery will be an important resource for those interested in healing, recovery, and wholistic perspectives of wellness. I am honored to be given the opportunity to contribute this foreword, and to be part of this meaningful work. I am confident this text will prove to be a useful roadmap as you walk the healing path, and as you walk alongside others on their healing journeys. The choice of two paths lay before us, we need only walk forward in a good way.

Kinanâskomitin / ᐲᓇᐋᐣᒡᑎᑊ / thank you,
Louis (Wawatewi Mistatim ᐄᐧᐄᐧᐁᐧᐃᐧ· ᒥᐣᑕᑎᐨ) Busch

—A hand-written signature

Preface

Beginning

Before you begin, we want you to know how we organized this book. Our goal is to blend our experiences, belief systems, academic training, research, and theories into one concise book that helps you endure well and begin or continue on a healing path. There is not just one path there are many paths and many readers. This is for you.

Each chapter begins with an introduction. In some cases, we present definitions of key terms that are used. We include theories based on the chapter content because theories are just our way of understanding the world. Stories from our own lives, friends, colleagues, and relatives contextualize healing from multiple perspectives. We are storytellers so in writing this book there were many Zoom calls, emails, and even a trip to Lander Wyoming in a cabin on a windy hill to set our intentions, and say our prayers, for this book. These show up as stories and conversations in the book. We call them **enduring well conversations** because that is what they were for us.

Chapter 1 This chapter introduces the text and provides a framework with visual drawings of a healing path based on the authors' own experiences and research. It describes the Five A's to walking on a healing path, awareness, acknowledgment, assessment, action, and apology. Clinical applications to healing from substance abuse and mental health disorders are presented along with theories and research that demonstrate current knowledge and evidence, and what is missing. Chapter 2 presents barriers that people encounter on the healing path. Depression, anxiety, and substance abuse are signs of not enduring well. This chapter describes the origins of depression, anxiety, and substance abuse and includes research and theories to help people heal. Chapter 3 chapter describes what trauma is, how people heal from trauma, and what individuals need to know about trauma on the healing path. Acute traumatic events, chronic traumatic events, collective trauma, historical trauma, and intergenerational trauma can impact our ability to heal and walk on a healing path. Using the

American Psychological Association definitions of trauma as a guide, this chapter compares how human responses to trauma are similar to animals hurt in the wild, the goal is to seek safety, support, and heal. Spirit is at the core of trauma, and some have described trauma as a hit to the spirit or soul. Chapter 4 presents the concept of recovery, how recovery happens, and common definitions of recovery. Authors draw on personal, spiritual, and clinical experiences to present a holistic approach to recovery. A critical point of recovery for many people is the recognition and understanding that we need to recover. Research, theories, and integrative approaches must be understood and accessed; this chapter describes spirituality, drumming, mindfulness, complementary alternative medicine, and art as pathways to healing and recovery. highlights systems that support recovery. Chapter 5 focuses on healing from trauma, substance abuse, and loss. Beginning with honor and healing, readers will understand the characteristics of healing people and the resources that heal. Qualities like optimism, self-esteem, social support, gratitude, and well-being are indicators that people are on the healing path. Spiritual paths are also discussed as the differences in beliefs and concepts about how people heal real-world examples of treatment program evaluations. Chapter 6 includes families on the healing path. Drawing on American Indian and Alaska Native families, the content also discusses the impact of historical grief, loss from boarding schools, and the impact of boarding schools on tradition, kinship systems, and healing. Children are at the center of all paths, but when trauma and substance abuse occurs, their lives are impacted, and their belief and confidence about the world are challenged. Healthy boundaries are at the core of family relationships and supporting other family members as they walk on a healing path. Chapter 7 is an invitation to the healing path. It summarizes opportunities, considerations, and contradictions of the healing journey. This is a process to understand and embrace the journey toward wholeness, balance, confidence, and peace. Walking through different faiths and ways of making sense of loss, death, and suffering, this chapter explores spirituality, relationships, and faith-based concepts. Living with and in contradiction and duality requires us to embrace, understand, and have patience and wonder with ourselves and the world around us.

Pedagogical Features

Every chapter begins with an introduction of key terms, then discusses theories, research, stories, clinical approaches, and practical tips for healing and enduring well. Stories are enduring well conversations between the two authors, noted by their first names. Resources listed at the end of each chapter provide more in-depth resources about the topics presented. References support the research and literature cited in developing each chapter.

Dee: I've been thinking … who would want to read this book. I mean why would anyone listen to me and what I have to say?

Allyson: Are you serious? Everyone wants to know what you have to say. You are a Native woman, a clinical psychologist, a grandmother, elder, mentor, researcher … why would someone not want to read this book is what I want to know … I was listening to Mitch Album talk about Tuesdays with Mori and what he learned through the writing process. This was not like our stories because you do not have a terminal illness and our conversations are based on trauma and addiction … and healing. But I cannot help but there are some similarities. There has been an urgency to capture what you think, at least from my perspective. In this I am the student, and you are the teacher. I can be full of stupid questions, and I feel no judgement about asking them. In any other place, I would be embarrassed to ask. But the kinds of things we are talking about in this book are not just based on academic training, PhDs, clinical work, they go beyond that you know.

Dee: Well that is true.

Allyson: And there is a spiritual force that is part of this writing, an unseen and indescribable feeling I've had while writing and visiting with you. We have just a week to submit this to the published. We are still writing and working on chapters. You told me we need more on trauma. I agreed. I started reading the literature and then realized I was late for teaching a class. Out of the blue, one student wanted to talk about trauma in Appalachia. She shared what it was like growing up, what happened in her family, the cyclical nature of trauma. We also talked about resilience, or post traumatic growth. This is what was missing from our chapter on trauma. So I had to believe in the Great Mystery, there was synchronicity in the writing process that would bring everything together. There have been other affirmations along the healing path too. For example, our ability to love and forgive everything is central to the healing path. I understand this more now that we have been writing about it. Also, the ability to seek out others who are on the healing path too, that is part of my walk. We have a connection, a similar experience, we are walking toward the same things. And service, giving to others with the expectation that we receive nothing in return. Teaching about social justice, public health, and dismantling oppressive systems. This is all part of the healing path. And the gifts we have and practice, and give if we are aware …

About the Authors

Dolores Subia BigFoot, PhD, is a child psychologist by training who holds the Presidential Professorship within the Center on Child Abuse and Neglect at the University of Oklahoma Health Sciences Center. Dr. BigFoot has over 30 years of experience and is knowledgeable about the concerns of implementation and adaptation of evidenced-based practices being introduced into Indian Country. Dr. BigFoot is an enrolled member of the Caddo Nation of Oklahoma with affiliation to the Northern Cheyenne Tribe of Montana where her children are enrolled members and the recognition that her children were raised in the Cheyenne traditions and ceremonies. Equity, inclusion, cultural identity, and belonging are values she promotes and practices. She values her role as mother, grandmother, sister, daughter, auntie, and mentor as being her calling and the pathway that brings others into the circles of cultural teachings. Her faith sustains her as she is a disciple of Christ. She was the wife of the late Cheyenne Chief and tribal historian John L. Sipe Jr. and the mother of C. Ah-in-nist Sipes and his siblings.

Allyson Kelley, DrPH, is a researcher, professor, author, and individual in recovery. She is the principal consultant and founder of Allyson Kelley & Associates PLLC (www.allysonkelleypllc.com). Allyson supports research, evaluation, training, and technical assistance efforts for several prevention, treatment, and recovery initiatives in the United States. Allyson earned her Master's degree in Public Health Practice from the University of Alaska Anchorage and her Doctorate in Public Health from the University of North Carolina at Greensboro. Allyson currently resides in the mountains of central Oregon. Her best day on a healing path includes teaching a class with public health students, time with family, gardening, and always lots of laughter.

Acknowledgments

We are grateful to the Creator, for the healing path we are on. Writing this was possible with the help and prayers of many. Family and friends, we love that you listened to our discussions on self-regulation, healing, forgiveness, and recovery. Louis Busch, Mayra Perez, and Kristine Litster Fales, your healing stories are at the heart of this work and give us reassurance and hope. Linda Donahue and Kaden Martin, your visual creations throughout this book bring the text to life. Brighten Crawford, we appreciate your help with interviews and transcripts. Angela Mize, you helped us find the time. We are grateful.

Chapter 1

Broken Spirits and the Healing Path

Healing

We need to redefine healing. Healing of the spirit is different than healing a physical wound. It is not even healing of the spirit, really. It is redefining experiences. This is how healing occurs in the spirit and the mind.

This book sheds light on various spiritual practices and clinical approaches used in a treatment setting. This book alone may not be enough for some people. Individuals with severe trauma histories, severe mental illness, and substance use disorders should seek professional help.

If You Are in Crisis Right Now, Living in the United States, Call or Text 988

John, my husband, died in January my son died in November. When John died I was no longer a wife, there was a term widow, then my son died, I was no longer a mom. What term is there? How do we bring those experiences in? What kinds of adjustments are necessary so that there is something on the other side? The healing of the spirit and the mind is not just healing, but it is somewhat transforming and evolving. Because you might not always have a scar that is visible but there is a transformation that takes place.

There are certain agreements we made about the healing path before we started writing.

Everyone is a spiritual being. The **spiritual pathway** is determined by the individual based on their own choice, insight, impressions, revelations, or other guidance from trustworthy, truthful, safe, and accurate sources. However, the fact that we are spiritual beings is not always measurable or evident such as with taking body temperature. In some cases, individuals may rely on intuition or similar constructs as a guide for making decisions about life. Where creativity, imagination, enthusiasm, humor, irony, motivation, desire, and yes, even intuition, evolves … this is our definition of being a spiritual being.

DOI: 10.4324/9781003274018-1

Heal, recover, renew, clarify, perspective, transition, restore, reclaim. These words are often used to explain what happens when there is a need to change for a better quality of life. Sometimes the **healing process** is referred to as treatment, therapy, counseling, rehabilitation, or psychotherapy; there are many terms. Different methods may be used, individual, family, couple, group, self-guided, or self-help with various delivery options such as virtual, web-based guides, in-person, homework-focused, retreats, solidary, and/or lectures with thousands in attendance. Healing may be totally secular, faith-based, or any perspective that resonates within the individual's worldview.

This book is opening the discussion on the heart-mind-body-spirit plus our relationships with self, others, and Creator. We talk about how brokenness occurs, what impact it has on the heart-mind-body-spirit, and how that impacts our relationship with ourselves, with others, with our sense of space ... which might be all of creation or our homes, that is our place in this world. Of course, the heart-mind-body connection is not new. Researchers have established that faith and prayer have positive impacts on our ability to find meaning and peace during challenging times (Yanez et al., 2009). In a practical sense, we must have an understanding of how our thoughts, faith, and beliefs impact our feelings or emotions. Action and behaviors determine our relationship with ourselves, others, and our surroundings ... and our ability to walk on the healing path.

Our discussions in this book explore how brokenness becomes part of our story and the process of healing. It is in the healing process that we become who we are meant to be. Brokenness can surface from many causes, our own sense of inadequacies, harm at the hands or voices of others, disappointments, unfulfilled expectations, natural disasters, man-made disasters, human frailty, misguidance by those who should know better, greed, revenge, control, or anything that presents a threat or harm ourselves or those that we love.

Society in general makes a lot of assumptions about self-sufficiency, independence, and making your own path. A pathway means that it is marked, someone else has walked on it, it is a way of assuring that someone has been there before, and they know the direction to go. This is reassuring. We are encouraging people to walk the **healing path**. Our lives are on a path. A path that is based on innate principles, beliefs, emotions, and experiences. We are spiritual beings. We learn to trust first, then love. We believe that we are inherently good. We believe in others. We have relationships that are important. We are born with gifts. Enthusiasm. Curiosity. Humor. Connection. Creativity. Imagination. On the healing path, these gifts are taken away, or buried by grief, loss, shame, addiction, or trauma. Everyone will experience trauma at some point in their lives, so understanding how to move through trauma and walk on a healing path during these times is a collective understanding that the world desperately needs. Without understanding, skills, or self-regulation practices, we tend to bury these emotions and feelings with unhealthy behaviors and relationships. Many numb these emotions and feelings with drugs and alcohol.

The ultimate message in this book and on the healing path is that we will experience trauma. But it is through trauma, pain, grief, loss, and suffering that we find healing and we support the healing of others. How we find the healing path is largely based on our choices and our belief systems. In this space of healing from trauma, grief, loss, and addiction, we can stand with the wound or pain in our spirit, acknowledge it, and move forward through it because we have a belief system and we have faith. For us, it is the belief in a higher purpose and a higher being. Some believe that brokenness is a struggle that is required to achieve Christlikeness or Creator likeness or self-actualization.

Understanding the impact of brokenness comes from an awareness of how harm and/or threats affect thoughts. What we say to ourselves, the stories in our heads, and feelings or emotions like sadness, depression, anger, hurt, or worthiness. These stories and feelings result in actions or behaviors. Behaviors are often fight, flight, freeze, or harm. Behaviors challenge our judgments about ourselves and the relationships we have with others. This understanding is important because each individual has five aspects of themselves.

- Thinking – cognitive, intellect, thoughts/dialogue in the head
- Affect – feelings, emotions, moods, temperament, passions
- Behavior – physical, gender, actions, doings
- Relational – social connections, family, friends, animals, humanistic, space, generational Spiritual – Great Mystery, God, Creator, religious or spiritual-based beliefs

We can anchor ourselves through balance and these five aspects of self. There will always be challenges to living in a world that is dynamic and unfolding. But there is also a positive interconnectedness between thinking, feeling, behaviors, relationships, and spiritual self that can lessen all brokenness and improve healing, recovery, hope, and joy.

Your life is built on the life of your ancestors, and the gift you give to them is in doing for future generations. There is always someone in the back of you and always someone ahead. Everyone wants a record of what happened. In the past and what will happen in the future. Because we learn through the experiences of others, your story will benefit future generations. This is your own story … your yesterday, today, and tomorrow. Your story is written while walking on the healing path. We can think about the healing path in terms of the **seven directions**, outward, in front, behind, beside, downward, inward, and upward. And the healing path also includes those who walk beside us, in front of us, and behind us.

It is impossible to live and not experience hardship. But it is in these times that we pivot, walk on a different path, or have an opportunity to forgive, heal, strengthen our faith, and find significance, meaning, and purpose, Figure 1.1.

Principles
We are inherently good.
We believe in others.
We learn to trust first, the love.
We have the gift of discernment, everyone.
We are spiritual beings.
We have relationships that are important.

Grace. Generosity. Service. Gratitude
Keeps Spirit
"Enduring Well"

Helps with processing space we are in. We are not buried in the trauma.

HEALING PATH

How do we enrich our gifts?

Gifts We Were Born With
Enthusiasm
Curiousity
Humor
Imagination
Connection
Creativity
Resilience

Trauma challenges faith

Figure 1.1 The Healing Path.

The Five As

When we were thinking about the healing path, the walk from brokenness to wholeness, we realized that there are five common things that people do when they experience a traumatic event, something that breaks them, or despair and suffering. Healing begins with awareness. Then moves toward acknowledgment, assessment, action, and apology. We will call this the Five As to Healing, and we will discuss these steps as a cyclical process because we are always healing and we are continually broken from the world that we live in and the space that we occupy.

Five As

1   Awareness – mindfulness, perceptions of self, healing intention, expectations, personal wholeness (body, emotions, thoughts, spirit)
2   Acknowledgment – truth, healing relationships, healing organizations
3   Assessment – observation, inquiry, symptoms, communication
4   Action – effort, coping, compassion, resilience, empowering beliefs, constructive behaviors, peaceful emotions, balance
5   Apology – letting go, forgiving self/others, release, reclamation, restoring (body, emotions, thoughts, spirit).

There are many ways of finding purpose, knowing how you arrived at the place that you are at and where you are going. We call this a **belief system**. You may have other ways to define this understanding, and that is okay. Our belief system is based on assumptions. Figure 1.2 presents our shared belief system, which is how we came to write this book, and the assumptions that guided our work presented here. Our beliefs are based on service to a higher being. We call this God or the Creator. Some believe in human service (e.g., Effective Altruism) or serving others. Others have beliefs based on service to themselves, and some do not believe in anything.

Figure 1.2 Belief Systems and Assumptions.

The terms faith, religion, and spirituality are often used interchangeably, and they have different meanings to different people. This is how we define these terms for this book. We realize that your definitions may be different based on your experiences, history, and worldview, and that is okay. **Faith** is a general attitude or set of personal beliefs. Faith is about the making, maintenance, and upkeep, and the transformation of human meaning (Fowler, 1986).

Fear and judgment are the reasons most people never talk about their spirituality or the idea that there is a spiritual aspect of our identity and space we occupy here on the earth, that is not merely physical. It is difficult to even name or measure. **Spirituality** is based on our connections, the principles that we live by, and what gives us meaning and purpose. Spirituality is a search for the sacred (Pargament & Exline, 2021). When we talk about spirituality, many people automatically think about religion. There are differences. **Religion** is about values, norms, statuses, roles, and groups. Religions tell their followers what is sacred and what is not (Newman, 2004). Religion often includes formal and organized groups, like Catholics and Buddhists. Practices such as reading the Bible, Book of Mormon, Torah, Quran, and more. Different religions have different ways of defining how we are spiritual or practice spirituality. For example, Christians may believe that their human spirit is transformed by the Holy Spirit. For example, John 4:42 reminds us that God is spirit and those who worship in him must worship in spirit and truth. Non-religious people can be spiritual, pray, meditate, or make conscious decisions informed by a spiritual presence or guide (Newman, 2004).

When we use the term **spirit** in this book, we are referring to a state of being. Spirit is at the core of who we are and our connection to the non-physical world, our spirit is who we are without our physical body. Spiritual healing comes from our beliefs about our purpose in life, how we find meaning, what we value, and our beliefs in a higher power. *Our spirit is at the center of all healing processes.* Spiritual healing is based on interactions and finding balance with interrelated practices like our behaviors, relations, thinking, and emotions, Figure 1.3.

There are foundational stakes of spirituality that must be discussed and recognized. We call these stakes but they could also be visualized as road barriers or signs that keep us on a healing path or walking in the direction that we want to go. We must consider where we are spiritually on the healing path before we consider how to heal and mend what is broken.

- What does spirituality mean to you? Do you embrace yourself as a spiritual being?
- Do you identify with a community or particular group on the healing path?
- Do you recognize that the healing path is spiritual, emotional, mental, physical, and relational balance? These are the interconnected aspects of us that are a process, not an end result.

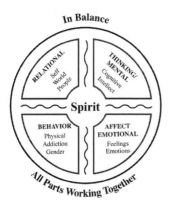

Figure 1.3 Our Spirit in Balance.

- Can you draw on others or family to utilize healing practices to work toward spiritual balance?
- How do you embrace enthusiasm for life, a sense of hope and joy, and a willingness to meet new challenges?

While there are many aspects of well-being and finding balance through spirit, **this book focuses on spiritual and clinical applications to healing from substance abuse and trauma**. This is what we know, what we have been trained to do, what our work is based on, and how we have walked on a healing path. This makes us qualified to share our ideas about healing with you. We also draw on previous creations like the Medicine Wheel (Lotzof, 2018), our work with mental health and substance abuse treatment programs (Kelley, 2022), and the Indian Country Child Trauma Center's principles and history. These combined helped us to conceptualize the healing and balancing process presented here.

Now we begin. This is not a traditional book. Much of the content comes from stories and discussions we have had about the healing path. There was a story about a young girl sitting under the kitchen table. She listened intently for several hours as her grandparents, aunts, and uncles told stories. I like to think that this book comes from under the table. Questions I have wanted to ask elders and wisdom keepers for a long time, but I just never had the opportunity. Dee is the elder or storyteller and I am the young girl under the table (Allyson).

Star People

Remember Stars Sill Shine Even when there is no Darkness.

Allyson: Over the years we have talked about being star people. I have mentioned this in some of my writings, or in conversations with people. It never goes as planned. Most people and readers have a difficult time accepting this or believing it. Where does the term star people come from and why is it so important to understand it on our healing path?

Dee: Different tribes have different stories. Many have stories about something happening, and people turning into stars and then they watch over the people, but science has shown us that nearly all parts of our body were made in a star, we are made out of star material (Lotzof, 2018). So, the stories that we have about origins have now been verified by science that we are star people. To understand who we are, where we came from, why we're here, and that we're star material, I think it's important if we can have our children and have each one of us recognize the essence of our place in this universe that we're not here by mistake.

We are Star People and we are from the stars. The Quill Work girl and her seven brothers are a Cheyenne Legend about a buffalo herd forcing these siblings into a tree. The siblings were too high up in the tree and feared they would never be able to return to earth. They turned into a star and became the Big Dipper. The brightest star is the sister who is filling the sky with quill work (First People, n.d.). The Bear Woman, A Blackfoot Legend is another. The incredible story of the Seven Sisters constellation (Pleiades) is another one. And the Kiowa legend of the Devils Tower is about seven girls being chased by bears. The girls found a rock and prayed to the rock to take pity on them and save them. The rock answered their prayers and grew taller and taller, pushing the girls higher and higher into the sky. The girls are now seven little stars in a group, the Pleiades. In the winter months, these seven stars shine brightly over Devils Tower. When people go to Devils Tower to look at the rock, they can see claw marks from bears all around the base (National Parks Service, n.d.)

The Great Mystery

Allyson: I love to hear your stories and thoughts. It is so completely different from what I have been taught to believe about who I am and where I came from. If we're star people and we are, then everyone in the world is a star person and pitiful at the same time, is that true? Every human? And so, they have that, capacity, or that magic, or have that connection to the Creator, that potential. And it's almost like a veil, and I'm just thinking out loud, but some people don't see that, or know that. And so, they stay in the place of being pitiful. Do we become star people by believing that we are star people?

Dee: I think again we're all spiritual beings and we're all social beings. And so, I think we have different levels of curiosity. My PhD dissertation advisor was adopted and he had no curiosity about his biological parents. None whatsoever. At least that he voiced. I mean he said he didn't search for them and or look for them, because he said his adoptive parents that raised him really shaped him. And that was who he was devoted to, that's who he saw as his parents. So, he didn't really have any curiosity about what was biologically before him. And I think for some people, you know that's true. He was a psychologist so of course you know he was very curious about people. I think there are just different levels of curiosity that cause us to search. And I think some people are not as curious about spiritual things. And some people aren't that curious about spiritual and social connections.

Allyson: When you are in a place of shame or addiction or when you're clouded, you are not curious. You are spiritually in a very different place. I guess I am trying to think about that because I agree, it's curiosity. But is there something more mystical? In your research and writing you always mention this entire space of the unknown, it's things we don't explain. Is that one of them we cannot put words to it?

Dee: There is that Great Mystery and things that we can't explain. I think we get evidence of it, but we don't always know how to explain it. The one story I tell is that I was home one evening, my son had just gotten his driver's license and I can remember sitting on the couch and I was doing something. And it was like six o'clock about 3:30 or 4:00 he had asked if he could go to the city of more, which is about seven miles away to pick up his friend and there were going to be two of them and he was going to come back and there was going to do something in Norman. And so, he had been gone for an hour and a half, and I was sitting there and a voice came into my head and it said, "You're going to get a call from an Oklahoma police officer, blah blah blah. The phone's going to ring and they're going to say, Mrs Sipes your son has been arrested and you need to come down to get him" and I was like, "Oh my goodness." And so, I sat there and about maybe 12 or 15 minutes later the phone rang and I said "hello" and they said, "Mrs. Sipes This is officer so and so and your son Sipes has been arrested and you need to come down." So, that Great Mystery. What was that? I can tell you what happened. I mean I can tell you what happened to me. I can tell you that I believed it, definitely. As soon as that came into my head, I believed that was it.

Allyson: Wow, that is really powerful. So, part of the Great Mystery is the voice that we hear, our intuition, telling us that something will happen.

Dee: Yes. I had to take my daughter to the emergency room and we lost her purse in the process. So, we said a prayer. And one of the attendants came in and said, "I just got this impression, you should just go check your car to see if her purse is in the car" and honestly, we swore up and down her purse was not in the car. I had a bigger bag and I had stuck her purse in my bag and totally forgot about it and had put it in the car and her purse was in the bag in the car.

How do we explain those things? So, there's that Great Mystery. It's working with us, it is not totally foreign. It's just that we can't explain it except that it's this Great Mystery. I mean I could say it's about our Creator, the spiritual side of us. I mean I know what comforts me, but that doesn't mean that what I say will convince somebody else. I only have evidence of what I can share in stories. But there is that Great Mystery that exists out there. Do we want to call on the Great Mystery or not?

Belief

Much of what we believe comes from our faith. Faith is what we have hope in and believe in. And Christians are still the predominant religious faith in the US. Christians make up about 63% of the US adult population, 6% identify with non-Christian faiths, 1% Jewish, 1% Muslim, 1% Buddhist, and 1% Hindu. Atheists or religious nones are increasing, with 4% of US adults describing their religion as "none" this is up from 2011 when 2% of US adults were nones. And, one in five adults claim a religion that is, "nothing in particular", this is an increase from 15% in 2011 (Smith, 2021).

Our spirituality and walk on the healing path are largely driven by what we believe. Our beliefs help us respond to adversity, weather the storms, and find trust in something bigger than ourselves. There are an infinite number of religions and beliefs that influence our walk on the healing path. For example, some cultures and religions believe that we should be punished for our sins and evil acts. Richard Rohr writes about this as a dualistic system of reward and punishment (Rohr, 2021). The ultimate punishment of non-belief is hell. But is that why we believe? So that we will avoid hell?

Allyson: Pastor Rob Bell's art exhibit about the search for peace in a broken world was highlighted on the front page of Time Magazine's April 2011 edition. The title was, "What if hell does not exist?" As a recovering evangelical, I read this and did not believe it. Of course, hell existed. I shared this with my conservative family members. I could not believe any pastor would even question the concept of hell. Bell criticized churches, saying that the only reason why they promote the concept of hell is that they want their parking lots to be full. Full of cars and bored, lost, broken souls, the church is their hospital. The church will save them from hell. Ten years have passed, it is 2022, and I think Rob Bell's article might have some truth. One of the stories that came from this article was a question about hell when someone left a note on an exhibit that said, "How do you know that John is in hell? Have you seen him there?" Are churches just hospitals that keep us from thinking we are going to hell?

Allyson: Today it was completely dark leaving Jackson Hole, Wyoming. The clouds and fog covered the landing strip, and the only light was runway strips and some lights on the airplane wing tips. It occurred to me that I have tremendous faith in the pilots, the airline, the engineers, the air traffic controllers, the gate agents, the fuelers, maintenance teams – everyone that keeps planes flying and in the air. I have not met them. Despite working for the airlines for ten years of my life, I know very little about how they can take off and land on a pitch-black morning before sunrise. Is this faith? For those of us who have grown up in the church or with a particular faith, we could apply these same ideas to our pastor, church, the bible, our parents, and Sunday school teachers. We believe what they tell us. We have faith that if we do what they tell us to do, then we will go to heaven and be rewarded eternally in heaven. But is this really why we believe?

One book that literally changed what I think about belief and life after death, or the final journey home is Eben Alexander's book, Proof of Heaven (Alexander, 2012). As a self-proclaimed atheist and trained neuroscientist, he believed that faith was just brain chemistry and that our souls were a product of this chemistry, and nothing more. But Alexander contracted a rare medical condition, he was in a coma for seven days. During this time, Alexander describes a slow spinning white light of great clarity associated with music, a subterranean real leading to a valley filled with colors and light that are not seen on earth. Moving through the valley, he describes his experience as a speck of awareness on a butterfly wing where thoughts of unconditional love and assurance were part of awareness. Alexander met an angelic being who took him to heaven. He met the Divine source of the universe itself, the Creator. Just as the doctors were considering stopping his treatment, he woke up. Now he believes in the Divine Creator of the universe. He has come to know, tell, and publish, that the brain does not create consciousness. He believes that we are conscious even without our brains. Alexander firmly believes that health, and I would add wholeness and enduring well, is only achieved when we embrace the Creator, the Divine, God. There are other stories too. A good friend died, went to heaven, and came back. The doctors pronounced him brain dead. During this time he transitioned into heaven. He told me about the colors in heaven, the bright light, and love, he did not want to return to earth. Another friend had a similar experience.

There are many spiritual, religious, and faith-based explanations and theories about why we should believe in the Divine. Eben Alexander's is just one. Explanations and stories are deeply personal, and closely mirror writing or discussing politics. I make it a point to never discuss politics because I realize that one's individual views about politics are their own, they are not mine, and they are not mine to change. People will vote, change, and believe based on their own journey, not a book, banner, or march. It is about choice. We must have conversations about beliefs on the healing path, God, suffering, and death. There are many contradictions, no matter what you decide to believe.

We are not experts on religion or dying. But we can tell you what different religions (beliefs) think about the end of physical life on earth. This understanding is essential in how we view the healing path. **Christians** (Protestants, Catholics, members of the Church of Jesus Christ of Latter-day Saints, and Orthodox Christians) believe that death is the separation of the eternal spirit from the physical body. Often when Christians are dying, a pastor or priest is called upon to perform rites, prayers, and sacraments. I think of the verse in Revelation 4:2, And immediately I was in the spirit, and behold, a throne was set in heaven, and one sat on the throne. And John 14:2, In my Father's house are many mansions: if it were not so, I would have told you. I go to prepare a place for you. **Jews** believe that death is a natural process and heaven is a place where pain and anxiety do not exist. **Islamists** believe that death is part of an overall divine plan of transitioning from the physical state of existence to a spiritual state of existence. **Buddhists** believe in reincarnation and karma. Individuals rebirth until they reach nirvana. **Hindus** believe that reincarnation occurs until one is freed from the death/rebirth cycle and enlightenment is attained. Those without religion. **Atheists and agnostics typically** do not believe in an afterlife, or that the soul or spirit survives. For some, these beliefs are rooted in a scientific understanding, that individuals are part of nature, and evolution, and have a specific role in the ecosystem, which ebbs and flows over time. Harvard University's newest spiritual leader and chaplain is an atheist. His work addresses the growing number of young people who do not claim a specific religion or believe in God and his mission is to unite and find common ground, in a humanistic way. **The contradiction here is that while people do not always believe in God, most Americans or 72% believe in heaven**. They believe heaven is a place where people who have led good lives are eternally rewarded," according to the Pew Research Center's Religious Landscape Study (2014).

Everyone's journey to the healing path is unique and driven by different beliefs and ideologies ... even thoughts about heaven and hell. Every person has a unique life experience, knowledge, and belief about what it takes to heal. We recognize these perspectives presented in this book are only our own. Much of what we know and write about in this book comes from our spiritual practices and the clinical world.

Allyson: What are your spiritual practices?
Dee: For me, prayer, scripture readings, being kind, having gratitude, having grace …

I have a mantra, grace, generosity, joy, and laughter. It is also about balance. How do we balance everything? It will never be perfect. How about your spiritual practices?

Allyson: Prayer, service, generosity, and peace. I pray before I go to bed, I listen to uplifting music, I find God in the forest, I see and seek the Divine in people. I love deeply. I attend the community church when life allows, I practice being authentic and truthful. I am still working on forgiveness.

Clinical applications are theories, research, interventions, treatment, and guidelines that are often used within a clinical setting. We realize that many readers have never stepped foot in a clinical setting. In fact, just 10% of adults with a substance use disorder ever seek clinical treatment (National Center for Drug Abuse Statistics, 2021). And, just 17% of adults received clinical mental health services in the last year (Substance Abuse and Mental Health Services Administration, 2019).

Faith and beliefs are related to science and theory. Faith is the principle of action and hope is the belief that by that action we will reach the outcome we desire. Conceptually we act and align with what our faith and hope are in, both to create and avoid certain things in life. What we have faith it can lead to our betterment or destruction (Allyson Kelley & Associates, 2022).

Science ---------Theory------------What we think will change

Faith--------------Beliefs------------What we hope will happen

A **theory** describes what we think will happen based on existing scientific evidence, research, experiences, and knowledge (Engel, 1980; Kelley, 2022). The use of theory in clinical practice helps build an evidence base about what is effective. Theoretically driven clinical treatment approaches are often tailored based on the target population and setting.

Clinicians use theories to diagnose, explain behaviors, or test assumptions about what is happening and what an individual needs to walk on a healing path. Sometimes the terms theory, model or framework are used interchangeably. Theories provide evidence, models are simplified explanations of theories, and frameworks are structures, systems, or plans with relationships (Kelley, 2022).

There are many **theories and frameworks** created to conceptualize spiritual healing. We will discuss these later in the book.

How Did We Get Here?

Layers of personal and institutional brokenness are evident everywhere that we look. Racism, discrimination, terrorism, wars, political division, and unrest are common. Power imbalances, differential access, limited resources, and sociocultural context impact how we view the world, and our walk on a healing path. Brokenness and detours on the healing path show up in our lives and the world in multiple ways.

- Lack of empathy
- Lack of family support/values
- Loss of faith, a crisis of faith
- Unresolved grief and loss
- Unhealthy coping
- Lack of self-regulation
- Lack of awareness

Allyson: Well, you talked about one of your husbands ... he was really strong in his faith, but then he had this other side. It makes me think about being star people but being pitiful there's always this kind of discrepancy between who we want people to think we are and who we are sometimes. And I wonder about that. I mean, there are all kinds of stories that we see, people falling from grace, medicine people, priests, elders, leaders, teachers ...

Dee: And you see it also in the creation stories because there's a lot of creation stories where there are twins, and one is doing one thing and one doing the opposite and there's this struggle. So, I think that there's always going to be a dichotomy there's always going to be ambivalence there's always going to be that different sides not only within us but in the world. And then appreciating that difference. We have that, we are star people and we're also pitiful. So, how do we help bring an understanding to that dichotomy, that conflict, which charge of how to be humble, how to be honored? And I think this is why people get very confused because, even within our bodies, we can have, it's fight, flight, freeze responses that have been there forever. And we can have all three of those responses in three seconds. We can look like we're charging, we can turn around, we can retreat. All of that is very immediate and it's not unusual, it's not out of the ordinary, it's just who we are and how we're built. And so, I think that recognizing there's not just one response is important. I don't know if I told you this but I have a friend, she has to go through 47 reactions before she gets to the right response and she knows that of herself now. She has trained herself, not to go with her first response because a lot of times if somebody tells us something we go, "oh no. how could that be?" and maybe we might go through one or two responses or even three or four responses, but to recognize that we need to go through 47 responses before we get to how we need to really react is pretty incredible. Most of us probably need to go through 8 or 9 or 10 or 12 before we get to a more honest or more thoughtful response.

And I think this is why a lot of people, especially our elders, don't say anything yet. We sit with it. Be quiet and let silence fill the time till you're ready to speak.

Research

Evidence from research tells us that many people are struggling to walk on a healing path (Kelley, 2022). We know that one in ten people globally lives with a mental health disorder (Ritchie & Roser, 2018). In the US, 8% of adults are in recovery from drug or alcohol problems and 13% of adults are in recovery from a mental health issue (National Survey on Drug Use and Health 2016, 2018).

Current systems, policies, and practices fail to support individuals, families, and communities on a healing path. The COVID-19 pandemic resulted in widespread grief, loss, and death. Researchers estimate that between March 2020 and April 2021, more than 1 million children in the world experienced the death of a parent, and children were five times more likely to lose a father than a mother (Kentor & Thompson, 2021). American Indian children were 4.5 times more likely to lose a parent or grandparent caregiver than non-Hispanic White children (Hillis et al., 2021). Some of these children will end up in the US foster care system, which results in intergenerational trauma. The foster care system is broken, and the outcomes of children moving through the system are less than desirable. People know this. But nothing has been done to fix the system. Broken systems lead to broken people. People that are far from the healing path. A review of 101 narratives from individuals involved in the foster care system revealed several themes, most importantly that the system does not support families or protect children as they experience difficulty (Greer, n.d.). This system clearly contributes to brokenness rather than wholeness. And this is just one system, there are so many systems that contribute to broken children, families, and generations.

Access to Healing Is Not Equitable

If walking on the healing path was an easy process, everyone would do it. Walking in honor. Walking as star people. But many people are stuck on the wrong path, they want to access the healing path but it seems so very far away. When we are stuck, we begin telling ourselves the wrong story … we are born into broken families, in countries where poverty is rampant, malnutrition is everywhere, war is common, and it is very difficult for some to walk on a healing path. We use the term **health disparities** to capture health differences that adversely affect historically marginalized groups. Health disparities are often grouped based on race/ethnicity, skin color, religion, or nationality; socioeconomic resources or position (reflected by, e.g., income, wealth, education, or occupation); gender, sexual orientation, gender identity; age, geography, disability, illness, political or other affiliation; or other characteristics associated with discrimination or marginalization (Braveman et al., 2011).

We have done a lot of work to promote healing from historical trauma, also called intergenerational trauma. **Historical trauma** with American Indian and Alaska Native populations has been called a soul wound, where the trauma is felt at a deep spiritual level. Experiences from colonization, assimilation, forced removal from traditional homelands, assimilation, and genocide have impacted generations on the healing path (SAMHSA, n.d.). Slavery in African American populations created trauma that continues today through racial injustice, oppression, and racism (Alim et al., 2008). The US has a significant and growing immigrant population, they often experience historical trauma due to forced relocation, migration, or displacement. Traumatic experiences continue in these populations due to discrimination, racism, and forced assimilation or acculturation. The cultural and spiritual practices of these groups are often threatened, creating stress and feelings of loss. Oppression and poverty stem from historical trauma and create conditions where access to a healing path is very difficult. Poverty in families, neighborhoods, and communities creates conditions where individuals are exposed to violence, victimization, abuse, retraumatization, and loss. Healing from historical trauma requires reparations, and restoration of culture, community, kinship, and relationships.

Not everyone has equal or equitable access to the healing path. This acknowledgment is at the core of our work, with communities who have been marginalized, discriminated against, and underserved. Our walk on the healing path is influenced by the past, present, and future, and our ability to live fully and completely on earth. How can we encourage people to walk on a healing path if their basic needs are not met? If they are hungry, poor, lack access to health care … healing seems far away. A ton of research has been done to investigate the reasons why some groups of people have worse health outcomes and difficulty finding the healing path (Kelley, 2020, 2022).

One of the greatest inequities on the healing path relates to housing and home ownership. How can we be on a healing path when our basic needs are not met? **Housing stress** which includes affordability, quality, stability, and loss of housing is related to feelings of brokenness. Stress related to living in poverty often contributes to psychopathology related to mental health and substance use behaviors and problems (Austin et al., 2021; Polcin et al., 2010). Individuals living in rural communities are more likely to report substance use disorders than more urban communities (Kelley, 2022, p. 202). For example, rural counties in the US report opioid prescribing rates and more deaths related to opioid overdoses. Social and environmental factors in rural locations may explain differences in higher rates. The normalization of prescription opioid use in rural communities increases use and overdose rates. Isolation, lack of treatment facilities, social and cultural norms, and stigma that may be associated with seeking treatment are also common (Bolinski et al., 2019).

Limited education and employment are barriers encountered on the healing path. Previous research indicates that the level of education achieved is directly linked to depression prevalence, where higher levels of education are associated with lower levels of depression (Henkel, 2011; Kelley, 2022). **Employment status** has been linked to depression, where individuals who are employed are less likely to be depressed than individuals who are not employed (Ritchie & Roser, 2018). An emerging body of research indicates that educational attainment, economic conditions, and substance use disorders are related, and countercyclical. While beyond the scope of this text, researchers documented the relationship between economic conditions, and factors like health insurance coverage, quality health care, risky health behaviors, poor diets, and drug and alcohol consumption patterns. **Socioeconomic status** (SES) impacts our ability to walk on a healing path. Researchers believe that SES predicts lifestyle choices and these choices often explain physical health and psychological health (Wang & Geng, 2019). In fact, individuals with lower SES are more likely to die from alcohol-related deaths than individuals with higher SES.

COVID-19 and the Healing Path

The **COVID-19 pandemic** disproportionately impacted historically marginalized groups. Hospitalization and death rates were highest among Hispanic patients, Black patients, and American Indian patients (Lopez et al., 2021). Reasons for differences are related to lower SES. During the COVID-19 pandemic, these groups were more likely to experience limited access to healthcare care coverage, overcrowding in their homes, travel on public transportation due to not having their own vehicle, and work in low-paying jobs that are in-person rather than remote. Immigrants were less likely to seek healthcare because they fear being deported or judged because they are using public services (Lopez et al., 2021). Substance use increased during the COVID-19 pandemic. Alcohol consumption during the pandemic ranged from 22% to 73% in the US general population. Mental health factors were the most common reasons for increased use of alcohol and other substances (Roberts et al., 2021). Alcohol consumption also increased during the pandemic among certain groups and characteristics. For example, living alone, being male, older age, parents with children at home, higher education, income loss or unemployment, poor physical health, fear and distress, impulsivity, and mental health conditions like depression, anxiety, hopelessness, and isolation. In comparison, risk factors associated with alcohol consumption before the pandemic were male gender, low levels of education, younger age, ethnicity (Hispanic or Black), existing mental health conditions, poor physical health, solitude, boredom, worry and fear, and a lack of social support.

What Now?

We must end this chapter on a high note, it's not all bad, even with COVID-19, addiction, trauma, inflation, climate change, and war. The healing path is really a shift in how we view ourselves and our surroundings. It is our mindset. It is establishing a more fulfilling identity about who we are and what we need to move forward in a good way, with honor. When we create negative identities that are reinforced by feelings of shame, guilt, despair, and anxiety, this limits our ability to progress forward on the healing path (Stavrova & Ehlebracht, 2019). We must deconstruct broken identities and create identities of hope, imagination, creativity, and meaning as the path forward. This is a spiritual and transformational process. By the last chapter of this book, our prayer is that you will have hope, you will walk as star people, strong in your identity and beliefs, and know that the healing path is possible and welcomes you in.

Practice on the Healing Path

- Think of a time that you have harmed someone.
- Did you feel guilt, shame, or broken?
- What actions did you take to make reparative actions toward this person?

When we harm someone, have past transgressions, feelings of guilt and shame. The healing path and process are about forgiveness, generosity, and love. It is feeling content and accepting of where we are at so that we can live fully, love wholeheartedly, and become the people we are meant to be. Human cruelty, loss, brutality, and mortality are part of life. But, with brokenness comes survival, losses are noted and strengths are established. Resilience can come from pain.

What are you willing to sit with?

Resources

Anxiety

Stanley J. Rachman, Routledge 2019, Rachman's in depth review of anxiety outlines the nature of anxiety, theories related to anxiety, related anxiety disorders, and treatment approaches. https://www.routledge.com/Anxiety/Rachman-Rachman/p/book/9781138311299?utm_source=cjaffiliates&utm_medium=affiliates&cjevent=94939a0d126511ed81869f160a1c0e14

Suicide Data and Statistics

Centers for Disease Control and Prevention, 2022. This website includes the prevalence of suicide, populations at greater risk and resources available. https://www.cdc.gov/suicide/suicide-data-statistics.html

Medicine Wheel

National Institutes of Health, 2022. This website includes resources on traditional uses of the Medicine Wheel and presents concepts of health and illness, https://www.nlm.nih.gov/nativevoices/exhibition/healing-ways/medicine-ways/medicine-wheel.html
988 Suicide and Crisis Lifeline, Call or text 988 if you are in crisis. https://988lifeline.org/

References

Alexander, E. (2012). *Proof of heaven: A neurosurgeon's journey into the afterlife.* Simon and Schuster: New York, NY, pp. 1–196.

Alim, T. N., Feder, A., Graves, R. E., Wang, Y., Weaver, J., Westphal, M., Alonso, A., Aigbogun, N. U., Smith, B. W., Doucette, J. T., Mellman, T. A., Lawson, W. B., & Charney, D. S. (2008). Trauma, resilience, and recovery in a high-risk African-American population. *The American Journal of Psychiatry, 165*(12), 1566–1575. https://doi.org/10.1176/appi.ajp.2008.07121939

Austin, A. E., Shiue, K. Y., Naumann, R. B., Figgatt, M. C., Gest, C., & Shanahan, M. E. (2021). Associations of housing stress with later substance use outcomes: A systematic review. *Addictive Behaviors, 123*, 107076. https://doi.org/10.1016/j.addbeh.2021.107076.

Bolinski, R., Ellis, K., Zahnd, W. E., Walters, S., McLuckie, C., Schneider, J., Rodriguez, C., Ezell, J., Friedman, S. R., Pho, M., & Jenkins, W. D. (2019). Social norms associated with nonmedical opioid use in rural communities: A systematic review. *Translational Behavioral Medicine, 9*(6), 1224–1232. https://doi.org/10.1093/tbm/ibz129

Braveman, P. A., Kumanyika, S., Fielding, J., LaVeist, T., Borrell, L. N., Manderscheid, R., & Troutman, A. (2011). Health disparities and health equity: The issue is justice. *American Journal of Public Health, 101*(Suppl 1), S149–S155. https://doi.org/10.2105/AJPH.2010.300062

Engel, G. (1980). The clinical application of the biopsychosocial model. *American Journal of Psychiatry, 137*(5), 535–544.

First People (n.d.). *The Quill-Work girl and her seven brothers—A CheyenneLegend.* https://www.firstpeople.us/FP-Html-Legends/TheQuill-WorkGirlAndHerSevenBrothers-Cheyenne.html

Fowler, J. (1986). *Stages of Faith, 1,* 342–348. http://images.acswebnetworks.com/1/2279/StagesofFaith.pdf

Greer, N. R. (n.d.). *Fostered Voices: Narratives of U.S. Foster Care.* Temple University. http://www.proquest.com/docview/2353043535/abstract/42E538CDC09D44BCPQ/1

Henkel, D. (2011). Unemployment and substance use: A review of the literature (1990–2010). *Current Drug Abuse Reviews, 4*(1), 4–27. https://doi.org/10.2174/1874473711104010004

Hillis, S. D., Blenkinsop, A., Villaveces, A., Annor, F. B., Liburd, L., Massetti, G. M., Demissie, Z., Mercy, J. A., Nelson III, C. A., Cluver, L., Flaxman, S., Sherr, L., Donnelly, C. A., Ratmann, O., & Unwin, H. J. T. (2021). COVID-19–Associated orphanhood and caregiver death in the United States. *Pediatrics, 148*(6), e2021053760. https://doi.org/10.1542/peds.2021-053760

Kelley, A. & Associates. (2022). *Theory of hope: Training worksheet* (pp. 1–6).

Kelley, A. (2020). *Public health evaluation and the social determinants of health* (Vol. 1–1 online resource (xi, 178 pages): illustrations, maps.). Routledge, Taylor & Francis Group. https://www.taylorfrancis.com/books/9781003047810

Kelley, A. (2022). *Treatment program evaluation: Public health perspectives on mental health and substance use disorders* (Vol. 1). Routledge.

Kentor, R. A., & Thompson, A. L. (2021). Answering the call to support youth orphaned by COVID-19. *The Lancet, 398*(10298), 366–367. https://doi.org/10.1016/S0140-6736(21)01446-X

Lopez, L., III, Hart, L. H., III, & Katz, M. H. (2021). Racial and ethnic health disparities related to COVID-19. *JAMA, 325*(8), 719–720. https://doi.org/10.1001/jama.2020.26443

Lotzof, K. (2018). *Are we really made of stardust?* https://www.nhm.ac.uk/discover/are-we-really-made-of-stardust.html

National Center for Drug Abuse Statistics. (2021). Drug abuse statistics. https://drugabusestatistics.org/

National Parks Service (n.d.) *First stories—Devils tower national monument (U.S. National Park Service).* https://www.nps.gov/deto/learn/historyculture/first-stories.htm

National Survey on Drug Use and Health 2016. (2018). *U.S. Department of Health and Human Services, Substance Abuse and Mental Health Services Administration.*

Newman, L. L. (2004). Faith, spirituality, and religion: A model for understanding the differences. *College Student Affairs Journal, 23*(2), 102–110. https://eric.ed.gov/?id=EJ956981

Pargament, K. I., & Exline, J. J. (2021). *Working with spiritual struggles in psychotherapy: From research to practice.* Guilford Publications. http://ebookcentral.proquest.com/lib/uncg/detail.action?docID=6733456

Polcin, D. L., Korcha, R. A., Bond, J., & Galloway, G. (2010). Sober living houses for alcohol and drug dependence: 18-Month outcomes. *Journal of Substance Abuse Treatment, 38*(4), 356–365. https://doi.org/10.1016/j.jsat.2010.02.003

Ritchie, H., & Roser, M. (2018). Mental health. *Our World in Data*. https://ourworldindata.org/mental-health

Roberts, A., Rogers, J., Mason, R., Siriwardena, A. N., Hogue, T., Whitley, G. A., & Law, G. R. (2021). Alcohol and other substance use during the COVID-19 pandemic: A systematic review. *Drug and Alcohol Dependence, 229*, 109150. https://doi.org/10.1016/j.drugalcdep.2021.109150

Rohr, R. (2021). *Breathing under water*. Franciscan Media.

SAMHSA. (n.d.). *Grants*. Retrieved October 22, 2021, from https://www.samhsa.gov/grants

Smith, G. A. (2021, December 14). About Three in Ten U.S. Adults are Now Religiously Unaffiliated. Pew Research Center's Religion & Public Life Project. https://www.pewresearch.org/religion/2021/12/14/about-three-in-ten-u-s-adults-are-now-religiously-unaffiliated/

Stavrova, O., & Ehlebracht, D. (2019). Broken bodies, broken spirits: How poor health contributes to a cynical worldview. *European Journal of Personality, 33*(1), 52–71. https://doi.org/10.1002/per.2183

Substance Abuse and Mental Health Services Administration. (2019). *2019 NSDUH Annual National Report | CBHSQ Data*. https://www.samhsa.gov/data/report/2019-nsduh-annual-national-report

Wang, J., & Geng, L. (2019). Effects of socioeconomic status on physical and psychological health: Lifestyle as a mediator. *International Journal of Environmental Research and Public Health, 16*(2), 281. https://doi.org/10.3390/ijerph16020281

Yanez, B., Edmondson, D., Stanton, A. L., Park, C. L., Kwan, L., Ganz, P. A., & Blank, T. O. (2009). Facets of spirituality as predictors of adjustment to cancer: Relative contributions of having faith and finding meaning. *Journal of Consulting and Clinical Psychology, 77*(4), 730.

Chapter 2

Depression, Anxiety, Suicide Ideation, Substance Abuse ... And Enduring Well

I cannot manage life; I cannot deal with sorrow. I cannot endure well. This is the story that many people tell themselves when they are feeling the brokenness of life, and the world is overwhelming. Brokenness often translates to depression, anxiety, suicide, shame, and despair, which can lead to substance abuse. Brokenness feels like a crisis of the spirit and a fear that life will not get better. The situation will not improve, and therefore hope is lost, joy is gone, and an escape is necessary.

Depression, Anxiety, Mental Health

Depression is experiencing bouts of sadness, sorrow, a sense of uncontrollable darkness, gloom, and worthlessness; there is no joy and there is no hope. The feelings are full of pain and heaviness.

This is what we know about depression. Depression is a mood disorder that causes symptoms that affect how we feel, think, or manage our daily lives. While everyone will experience a depressed mood for a variety of reasons, there are chronic and acute types of depression that can overlap. The difference with depression is that the symptoms must be present for at least two weeks. Depression is caused by genetic, biological, environmental, and psychological factors. Risk factors include a personal or family history of depression, life changes like trauma or stress, and certain illnesses or medications (National Institutes of Mental Health, 2022).

We are finally seeing the light after the global pandemic of COVID-19 and the devastating effects of unexpected loss, isolation, fear, chronic health impacts, job and housing loss, little or no control, and more. More than 21 million adults (8% of the population) in the United States experienced at least one major depressive episode in 2020. Rates were higher among females, with 11% of females and 6% of males reporting a major depressive episode. Individuals between 18 and 25 are the most likely to experience a depressive episode, representing 17% of all cases. Individuals reporting multiple races experienced the highest rates of depression (Substance Abuse and Mental Health Services

DOI: 10.4324/9781003274018-2

Administration, 2021). A global study pointed to a 28% increase in major depressive disorders and a 26% increase in anxiety disorders during the pandemic (COVID-19 Mental Disorders Collaborators, 2021, p. 19).

Depression was the most common risk factor associated with increased alcohol use during the pandemic (Roberts et al., 2021). And online alcohol purchases increased 477% during this time (Nielsen IQ, 2020). A review of 12 studies suggests globally that depression increased seven times greater than pre-pandemic levels (Bueno-Notivol et al., 2021).

Depression during COVID-19 Pandemic – 25% (range 18% to 33%)

Depression before COVID-19 Pandemic – 3% (range 2% to 6%)

(Bueno-Notivol et al., 2021; Ritchie & Roser, 2018)

There are different types of depression and causes, beyond the COVID-19 pandemic. In a clinical setting, here is how depression is characterized and defined. **Persistent depressive disorder** (also called dysthymia) is persistent, lasting for at least two years. **Postpartum depression** is experienced by many women after giving birth. Women with postpartum depression experience full-blown major depression during pregnancy or after delivery. **Psychotic depression** occurs when a person has severe depression plus some form of psychosis, such as having disturbing false fixed beliefs or hearing or seeing upsetting things that others cannot hear or see. **Seasonal affective disorder** occurs during the winter month there is less natural sunlight. **Bipolar disorder** is different from depression, someone with this disorder may experience episodes of extremely low moods that meet the criteria for major depression (called "bipolar depression"). One of the differences with bipolar disorder is that individuals experience extreme high – euphoric or irritable – moods called "mania" or a less severe form called "hypomania" (National Institutes of Mental Health, 2022).

Theories of Depression

We use biological and psychological theories to explain and understand depression in clinical settings, research, and training. While we will not review all of them, here are a few. **Psychological theories** have found that the risk of depression increases with physical and emotional changes affecting the central nervous system. These influence functioning, lack of supportive networks and poor relationships, and not being socially integrated into a community or society (Wasserman, 2011). The **cognitive theory of depression** claims that cognitive distortions contribute to depression. The **Cognitive Triad** developed by Aaron Beck presents three thinking patterns that lead to depression: 1) negative self-view, 2) negative and hostile perception of the world, and 3) negative expectation that future suffering and failure are inevitable (Beck & Beck, 1979). **Biological theories** are also used to explain the causes of depression, for example, the interaction and balance between neurotransmitters is a critical factor in mood regulation and depression.

Anxiety and Fear

Dee: Our key message about anxiety is that it is real. It has different origins. People think they cannot do anything about it, but the majority of the time we can decrease it considerably. We may not recognize it all of the time. Anxiety can manifest itself in different ways.

Anxiety is a tense unsettling anticipation of a threat, a feeling of uneasy suspense (Rachman, 2019). The negative emotional state one feels from anxiety is closely related to fear. One distinction between the two is that fear relates to a perceived threat or danger, like a bear attack. Fear typically goes away with time or when the source of danger is limited, but anxiety may persist and surface unexpectedly without any threat. **Social anxiety** and **social phobias** are terms used to describe a feeling of intense discomfort and avoidance in social situations. **Panic disorders** are repeated episodes of intense fear that often occur unexpectedly. **Agoraphobia** is the fear of being in public places where escape is difficult.

Allyson: When we go to the restaurant with Jane, she must sit in the seat closest to the exit. She is afraid there will be a fire, or something will happen in the restaurant that traps her in there with no way out.
Dee: Yes, specific phobias may be related to a specific object or experience, airplane travel, being in an elevator, or bees. I have seen that a lot.

Obsessive-compulsive disorder is another anxiety disorder that consists of repeated and intentional events.

Allyson: Several years ago, a friend and her family came to stay at our house. I had never spent much time with her oldest child but I knew they experienced obsessive-compulsive disorders. They washed their hands repeatedly and turned the faucet on and off. This behavior also occurred with the door locking mechanism at the front entryway and unlock, lock and unlock.
Dee: This must have been difficult for their family. Most of the world does not understand the underlying reasons for these behaviors.

Generalized anxiety disorder (GAD) is characterized by ongoing and excessive worry.

Allyson: One of my relatives experiences GAD; they unrealistically worry about a man kidnapping their children. While multiple types of anxiety disorders exist, the one thing they all have in common is that they are characterized by fear and or a negative emotional state. When we are in a place of fear and negative thoughts it is difficult to find the healing path.

Anxiety often co-occurs with other mental health and substance use problems, for example, depression. A study of adults diagnosed with depressive disorder found that 45% to 67% also experienced anxiety (Kircanski et al., 2017). A review of 29 studies from 80,879 youth across the world during the COVID-19 pandemic reported that 25% of youth reported depression and 21% anxiety (Racine et al., 2021). Many individuals self-medicate with substances to manage their anxiety. **A review of empirical literature found that anxiety disorders occur before substance use disorders in at least 75% of cases** (Kushner et al., 2008). However, this results in more challenges where one disorder exacerbates the other (Smith & Book, 2008).

Allyson: When I read the review of 75 studies on anxiety, I finally found some peace … I see the reasons why people cannot stop using. My grandfather was anxious and experienced mental illness, during World War II; he was not accepted into the draft. With limited resources or knowledge about his illness, he began to drink, heavily, and violently, until he took his own life at the age of 51.

Dee: That is tragic.

What Places People at Risk for Anxiety?

Age, gender, education, and marital status may determine your risk for anxiety. Although anxiety has always been around, today we live in a world with immediate and ongoing access to information, which creates more anxiety. Researchers explored anxiety trends in US adults from 2008 to 2018, and reported rapid increases in anxiety in young adults (Goodwin et al., 2020). Adults under age 50 in the US are experiencing the greatest increases in anxiety, researchers believe that this is related to direct and indirect exposure to anxiety-provoking events on social media. Women are more likely to experience anxiety than men, and individuals with an income lower than $20,000 per year experience the highest rates of anxiety. Marital status also relates to anxiety, where adults who have never been married experience higher rates of anxiety than those who have been married. Education also plays a role in anxiety, individuals without a high school diploma reported higher rates of anxiety than other groups with higher education levels.

Doctors are trained to respond to something. You go to the doctor for anxiety. They want to give you pills. They never ask you why you are feeling the way you are feeling.

Treatment of anxiety may include pharmacotherapy and medications such as Paxil or Zoloft. Psychotherapies are also used to treat anxiety disorders and substance use disorders. Cognitive-behavioral therapy (CBT) is effective in the treatment of anxiety disorders and may be more effective for individuals with both substance use disorders and anxiety (Smith & Book, 2008).

Allyson: I am struck by how much anxiety shows up in all of this. In our work, recovery, addiction, harming of self and others. I want to know why I am anxious and what I need to do about it, without drugs or alcohol. Is that possible?

Dee: It is a feeling that people have with themselves and with other people. It has been recognized for thousands of years. It is in the Bible, it is a God-given trait. It is a God-given trait because it is in the scripture. When we think about anxiety, we think it is always bad. Some anxiety is good, it gets you motivated. For some high anxiety is how they live their life, they learn how to navigate with high anxiety. The other part of this, you turn on the switch, and they don't know how to turn it off. Hormones, environment.

It says and we know that the body remembers me so, having information about how the body remembers, how the mind works that is that process to better manage today and future things. So, if we have anxiety attacks and we don't know how to manage that, what do we do? Youth body's reaction doesn't have anything to do with anything you're thinking and all of a sudden you just have an anxiety attack ... the body does remember, but when you know feel it, what can you do? I have anxiety and it's not a new thing, but it's manageable and it's honest and it is sometimes an excuse, so I can get myself together again. So, I can figure out how to mauver through whatever circumstance. And it's also about disappointment when you have anxiety. It's like are you going to go through with this or not ... and if you don't how disappointed are you going to be? So, it's not dismissing the body, but it is figuring out how do you manage. Mastery is really really really key. It's knowing what your triggers are so that you can master whatever reactions you're having. You might not necessarily know it at the time, but you can figure it out, and then, even if you've done something to disappoint someone or harm someone, then you learn forgiveness. How do you help navigate that forgiveness and forgiving of self and forgiving others and asking for forgiveness? So, I think if we think about all of this when we think about that brokenness, it's because we are social beings and other people are important to us.

Theories on Anxiety

Anxiety has been studied for nearly 100 years. This has resulted in multiple biological and psychological theories about anxiety. Some theorize that anxiety is a learned behavior, while others point to genetic or biological causes. Relating to **biological theories** of anxiety, some believe that anxiety is the result of a deficiency in serotonin metabolism. This theory has resulted in an increase in selective serotonin reuptake inhibitors (SSRIs) to treat a variety of anxiety disorders. But, researchers relying heavily on a biological theory and the use of SSRIs have failed to fully explain the biological causes of anxiety disorders with biochemical explanations (Rachman, 2019). **Genetic theories** are also used to explain anxiety, predominantly epigenetic theories, which focus on how environmental factors shape overall disease risk by changing our genetic makeup that contributes to anxiety disorder risk genes (Domschke & Maron, 2013). Traumatic brain injury and hormones are often cited in theories related to anxiety.

Dee: After the Oklahoma City bombing people's anxiety increased, they were watching the news 24 hours a day. Or another example is, with storms, every channel starts broadcasting 24 hours a day. People will say I am turning this off, I cannot take this. The constant information … On the other hand, there people's anxiety is so high that by listening all of the time, they feel like they can control it. Anxiety has shifted our way of making sense of the world.

Some people's genetic code is that they have high anxiety. It exacerbates when things are going on. When there is a lack of control, unexpected events can create anxiety. Anxiety has always been with us. In the bible, it says I am anxious for you. How do we use that God-given trait? We have God-given traits in terms of artists, music, and discernment. Anxiety can be good. We anticipate things … a kid going to Disneyland. I can't wait for … . People will pay to be anxious. Alfred Hitchcock, his entire world was around suspense. We pay for it, we give hard-earned money to get this tension in our bodies, over and over again. These are under controlled conditions and limited. When we don't have control, we don't know the limits, and it is difficult. We have to be vulnerable. In public speaking, anything that calls attention can create anxiety. Vomiting, passing out, sweaty palms. Anxiety is part of PTSD. Learning how to physically maintain your sense of grounding is a skill. That is mastery. I know what this is. I know what is going on. People drink, they have high anxiety, and they want to remove it. We teach therapists all of the time to teach grounding and relaxation skills. The therapists will have these anxiety attacks. You are teaching a 6-year-old kid to practice these things to address their anxiety.

Therapists may teach it but they don't believe in it or practice it. That is a problem.

Allyson: What has been your experience with your own anxiety and how have you managed it?

Dee: I don't see myself as an anxious person. But when I was pregnant with my son, I was having out-of-body experiences. If we have anxiety attacks and we don't know how to manage that ... its difficult. When you know and you feel it, what can you do? I have anxiety and it's not a new thing, but it's manageable and it's honest and it is sometimes an excuse, so I can get myself together again. So, I can figure out how to mauver through whatever circumstance. And it's also about disappointment when you have anxiety it's like, are you going to go through with this or not, and if you don't how disappointed are you going to be? So, it's not dismissing the body, but it is figuring out how do you manage. And with Gathering of Native Americans, it's about interdependency, it's about generosity, it's about mastery. I think mastery is really key. It's knowing what your triggers are so that you can master whatever reactions you're having, you might not necessarily know it at the time, but you can figure it out, and then, even if you've done something to disappoint someone or harm someone, then you learn we're forgiveness comes into that and how do you help navigate that forgiveness and forgiving self and forgiving others and asking for forgiveness? So, I think if we think about all of this when we think about that brokenness, it's because we are social beings and other people are important to us, that we experience anxiety.

Suicide

Suicide is becoming more and more common and the US and Canada have some of the highest rates of suicide in the world (WHO, 2019). In 2020, 44,834 people in the United States died by suicide and 1.2 million people aged 18 or older attempted suicide (Substance Abuse and Mental Health Services Administration, 2021). Suicide rates increased by 36% between 2000 and 2018 and declined by 5% between 2018 and 2020. Rates are higher among racial and ethnic minority groups. For example, American Indian Alaska Native groups have some of the highest suicide rates in the nation (Ramchand et al., 2021). Suicide and suicide attempts often occur more frequently in people with schizophrenia (Siris, 2001). Depression and stressful life events often contribute to suicide ideation (Kelley et al., 2018). Environmental factors also increase the risk of death by suicide. Depression and alcohol use disorders have been linked to suicide, especially in high-income countries like the US. Crisis, financial problems, relationships, and health problems increase suicide risk (WHO, 2019). This finding is consistent with a lot of the research we have done on early mortality from chronic diseases like diabetes, to the prevention of substance misuse, and long-term recovery. Employment keeps on showing up as a significant supporter of the healing path.

Research and Theories on Suicide

A review of recent research calls for increasing social welfare expenditures and policies to assist low-income individuals, restricting firearm and alcohol availability, promoting parenting and marriage (both are protective), and creating opportunities for social support, better mental health, and better physical health (Stack, 2021). What if the answer to reducing suicide risk was job training, job skill, and vocational development programs and opportunities? We rarely see these are prevention or interventions, we often see the individual at risk, the person at the clinic, or sometimes the individual when it is too late. Males continue to complete suicide at higher rates than females. The strongest factors that predict suicide are low SES and unemployment. Increasing the minimum wage by just $1 decreased suicide rates by 6% in one national study (Kaufman et al., 2020).

One of the most widely used theories about suicide was developed by Thomas Joiner. His work, the **interpersonal-psychological theory of suicidal behavior**, tells us that an individual will die by suicide if the desire and capability to act on that desire converge (Ribeiro & Joiner, 2009). An individual's **mind and body factor** into suicide risk and suicide completion. A review of studies and clinical data indicates that the following mind/body factors increase risk: depression, mental illness, being abused or mistreated, self-injury, impulsivity, major physical illness, mood disorders, and previous suicide attempts. **Environmental factors** also increase risk. Barriers to mental health services, lack of community support, homelessness, death or relationship breakups, job loss or change in financial security, feeling unsafe, family history of suicide, high-stress family environment, family or school crisis, and easy access to lethal materials. Risky behaviors, lack of support, beliefs that suicide is a solution, exposure to suicide through media and friends, not being willing to seek help, non-suicidal self-injury, victimization, and bullying are also factors that contribute to suicide. Efforts to **lower suicide risk** include quality competent healthcare from medical and mental health professionals, healthy coping, problem-solving, and conflict resolution skills, restricted access to lethal means, strong connections with family, safe environments, non-violence, acceptance, safety, support, self-esteem, and connection.

Dee: Suicide can be connected concentrically. It does not take much to feel like I am doing great and I want to kill myself. Or my life is not worth living. I am in so much pain I cannot stop all of these thoughts. With paranoia and schizophrenia, individuals believe they were told to do so something. A lot of times people don't discern the voices in their heads.

Allyson: How do you know if the voices in your head are schizophrenia or something else?

Dee: My nephew died in Colorado about five years ago. It was before the pandemic. I knew it was hard for me to drive at night due to declining night vision. A common decline as one ages, however, to arrive on time I needed to help drive. It's a 15-hour drive. With my turn driving, it was the middle of the night, straight, flat 4-lane interstate, a very isolated rural highway without much scenery. When I was driving in the middle of the night with darkness all around, my visual perception saw canyon walls, looming tree branches, and shadows and forms that kept skipping past my line of vision if I tried to catch them by trying to locate the image. Because of glaucoma, I have nighttime driving issues. All of these things I could see, it was in the peripheral of my vision, and forms, figures, and shapes danced along as images that were not quite discernible but quite noticeable if I focused on them. If you did not realize it was glaucoma, a condition that deteriorates your night vision and not letting sufficient light get through to your rods and cones ... you might think it is schizophrenia and become paranoid. You could also become confused and think that no one was listening to you as you shared these thoughts and perceptions. But I knew what it was so I could dismiss it and not be concerned about imagery and visual images.

I have hearing loss. There are sounds that exist due to hearing lost. I hear things that no one else can hear. If I did not know it was tendonitis and hearing loss effects, I would think, oh my goodness is someone talking? I could create a lively conversation that is not real. When there is triggering in the senses, the tendency is to jump to a conclusion, which is what you tend to believe. I had eye surgery, I see much better but I have floaters and light bubbles. I go to sleep and wake up and see a light in my eye. I see things out of the corner of my eye that are floaters, I might think that someone just walked by or we have mice in the house. There is a tendency to interpret conditions of sight, sound, and smell ... For some things, there are biological explanations, but if you don't know that you can appear to be paranoid or unreasonable and challenging.

Allyson: One of the projects we worked on together was a 10-year youth suicide prevention effort. I recall working with an elder and knowledge keeper to really understand what suicide meant in their community, I quickly realized that their definitions of suicide, what it was, why it happened, and what it meant were very different from my western-trained textbooks. They viewed suicide as a spirit that comes to help those in spiritual pain, and it is also a spiritual guide that comes to listen and help individuals in their times of need. One community member talked about spirit is and how it can be used as a way to help the people. We worked to help others understand, so they could start healing their own pain and listen better to the spirit being called to their community (Kelley et al., 2015). This belief and way of thinking about suicide was radically different from what I knew, and I embraced it.

Three years later we published another paper about this project and documented the risk and protective factors of suicide ideation in this community. The interpersonal theory of suicide guided this research; when individuals perceive themselves as a burden and do not belong, this is sufficient to cause suicide. We studied social support, self-esteem, depression, anxiety, stress, and suicide ideation with 100 youths. We found that depression alone was the strongest risk factor for suicide ideation. Depression was also correlated with stressful life events, and stressful life events were associated with anxiety. Females had higher suicidal ideation scores than males and reported lower self-esteem (Kelley et al., 2018). Females continue to be at greater risk for suicide ideation but more males complete suicide than females.

Dee: Yes, I remember this work.
Allyson: What saddens me is that the work ended, we did not get to do enough to intervene, people died from suicide in this community. They could not find a way to the healing path.

Self-Harm and Cutting

Self-harm is a major mental health issue, but it does not mean an individual is suicidal. Clinicians and researchers report that it is motivated by a desire to regulate feelings, of tension, or sadness (Millard, 2015). Most people who engage in self-harm or cutting are not suicidal, historically clinicians diagnosed them with a borderline personality disorder (identified by unstable moods, impulsivity, and problematic relationships). However, researchers report that most people who engage in self-harm do not have borderline personality disorder (Masterson, 2010).

Allyson: Why do people intentionally cut or burn themselves? I have seen this a lot with the students and youth that we work with.
Dee: This goes toward managing emotional pain, easing emotional pain. Not all cutters are suicidal and not all cutting is a precursor. There is

great shame around cutting, people try to hide it. Not all cutting is a mental health crisis. Mental health issues are environmental, organic, chronic or long-term, and some are time limited. We tend to treat them all the same. And that is not the right approach.

Substances and Substance Use Disorders

Substance use and misuse are part of human history. Archaeological findings from 7000 to 5000 BC suggest that alcoholic beverages were consumed by humans then. Human use of poppy plants and hemp fibers has been traced back more than 6,000 years ago (Escohotado, 1999). When we think about substance misuse we should think of it as a less-than-ideal way of coping and poor self-medicating skills. Gabor Maté states that the majority of addiction is due to experiencing trauma which is the focus of his book, In the Realm of Hungry Ghost (Maté, 2008). We will review more about trauma and substance misuse in chapter 3.

When we use the term substance, this is any psychoactive compound with the potential to cause health and social problems, including addiction. Substances may be legal like alcohol or tobacco, or illegal like heroin and cocaine. Some substances are prescribed for medical purposes, like hydrocodone or oxycodone (e.g., Oxycontin, Vicodin, and Lortab) (Kelley, 2022). These substances are often categorized based on their pharmacological and behavioral effects (McLellan, 2017).

Here is a list of substances that are often misused:

- Nicotine – cigarettes, vapor cigarettes, cigars, chewing tobacco, and snuff
- Alcohol – including all forms of beer, wine, and distilled liquors
- Cannabinoids – marijuana, hashish, hash oil, and edible cannabinoids
- Opioids – heroin, methadone, buprenorphine, oxycodone, Vicodin, and Lortab
- Depressants – benzodiazepines (e.g., valium, librium, and xanax) and barbiturates (e.g., Seconal)
- Stimulants – cocaine, amphetamine, methamphetamine, methylphenidate (e.g., Ritalin), and atomoxetine (e.g., Stratera)
- Hallucinogens – LSD, mescaline, and MDMA (e.g., Ecstasy)

Most people who use drugs do not become addicted to them (Volkow et al., 2017). What contributes to differences in addiction status is an individual's susceptibility based on genetic, environmental, and developmental factors that are largely out of a person's control. Researchers have found that individuals are more likely to develop a substance use disorder if they have a family history, early exposure to drug use, exposure to high-risk environments, and certain mental illnesses (Stanis & Andersen, 2014; Volkow et al., 2017). We will talk more about these risk factors throughout this book.

The **American Psychiatric Association (APA)** maintains the Diagnostic and Statistical Manual of Mental Disorders **(DSM-5)**, which is used to create labels, diagnose, and treat substance use disorders. Diagnosis of substance use disorder may involve a physical exam, lab tests, and psychological evaluation. The DSM-5 recognizes substance use disorders resulting from the use of 10 separate classes of drugs: alcohol; caffeine; cannabis; hallucinogens (phencyclidine or similarly acting arylcyclohexylamines, and other hallucinogens, such as LSD); inhalants; opioids; sedatives, hypnotics, or anxiolytics; stimulants (including amphetamine-type substances, cocaine, and other stimulants); tobacco; and other or unknown substances. Importantly, diagnosis is the driver for insurance payment, treatment, and levels of care (Kelley, 2022). Clinicians often use the following criteria to diagnose a substance use disorder:

- Taking the substance in larger amounts or for longer than you're meant to.
- Wanting to cut down or stop using the substance but not managing to.
- Spending a lot of time getting, using, or recovering from use of the substance.
- Cravings and urges to use the substance.
- Not managing to do what you should at work, home, or school because of substance use.
- Continuing to use it, even when it causes problems in relationships.
- Giving up important social, occupational, or recreational activities because of substance use.
- Using substances repeatedly, even when it puts you in danger.
- Continuing to use, even when you know you have a physical or psychological problem that could have been caused or made worse by the substance.
- Needing more of the substance to get the effect you want (tolerance).
- Development of withdrawal symptoms, which can be relieved by taking more of the substance (American Psychological Association, 2020).

The DSM-5 allows clinicians to determine the severity of the substance use disorder based on the number of symptoms identified. Substance use disorder is defined in the DSM-5 as a maladaptive pattern of use characterized by 2 (or more) of 11 symptoms listed above (Martin et al., 2011). Two or three symptoms indicate a mild substance use disorder; four or five symptoms indicate a moderate substance use disorder, and six or more symptoms indicate a severe substance use disorder. Other options for clinicians when diagnosing a substance use disorder include "in early remission," "in sustained remission," "on maintenance therapy" for certain substances, and "in a controlled environment" (American Psychiatric

Association, 2013). A diagnosis of substance use disorder is not all bad, it's actually the first step in addressing the problem so that people can actually walk toward a healing path.

Barriers to the Healing Path

Barriers on the healing path are part of a larger body of literature on public health, social justice, and advocacy. Here are some factors that increase risk and contribute to poor treatment and healing outcomes: sex and gender roles, age, trauma, housing stress, rural community location, education, employment, and socioeconomic status.

Sex and gender roles matter when it comes to understanding the prevalence and treatment of substance use and substance use disorders. **Sex** refers to one's physiological structures and sex assigned at birth as male, female, or intersex (Gilbert et al., 2018). **Gender** is a social construct that includes how we feel, act, behave, see the world, and interact with others (Grant et al., 2015). Substance use and substance use disorders vary by gender, for example, men are more likely to be diagnosed with an alcohol use disorder than women (Schick et al., 2020). Research on gender minority populations, which include transgender, gender non-binary, gender-queer, and other gender non-conforming groups has found that binge drinking is higher among transgender populations, especially in early adulthood (Schuler et al., 2018). Consequences related to substance use disorders are more common and more severe among gender minority populations, for example, stigma, discrimination, and negative attitudes about gender identity have been linked to transgender-related issues (Gilbert et al., 2018). Other special population subgroups that experience higher rates of substance use and substance use disorders include homeless individuals, prisoners, veterans, and sex workers (Aldridge et al., 2018).

We also know that an individual's **age** when they first use a substance is associated with an increased risk for problematic substance use and substance use disorders (Richmond-Rakerd et al., 2017). Most individuals with a substance use disorder started using before they were 18 and developed a disorder by age 20 (Dennis et al., 2002). Researchers have found that 15.2% of people who begin drinking before the age of 14 will develop alcohol abuse or dependence. In contrast, just 2.1% of individuals that wait until they are 21 or older to begin drinking will develop alcohol abuse or dependence (Richmond-Rakerd et al., 2017). The rate is higher for prescription drug use where 25% of individuals who begin abusing before age 13 will develop a substance use disorder in their lifetime. Marijuana is the most common substance used in early adolescence and 13% of individuals with a substance use disorder began using marijuana before they were 14 (Dennis et al., 2002). Researchers report differences in substance use patterns based on age and race, African American individuals initiate alcohol use at older ages and engage in less underage drinking than Whites (Zapolski et al., 2014).

Substance use and substance use disorders are often the symptom or result of unresolved trauma. **Exposure to trauma**, especially during childhood is associated with substance use disorders. Research from a national survey of youth reports that those who experienced physical abuse or sexual abuse and assault were at least three times more likely to report abusing substances compared to other youth without trauma histories (Funk et al., 2003). Researchers found that 70% of youth receiving treatment for a substance use disorder also had a history of trauma (Khoury et al., 2010).

Where we live impacts how we live and our overall health, including substance use and substance use disorder. **Housing stress** which includes affordability, quality, stability, and loss of housing is related to substance use disorder (Kelley, 2022). We have studied the reasons why substance use occurs using the **social causation hypothesis** as a guide, where stress related to living in poverty often contributes to psychopathology related to substance use behaviors and problems (Austin et al., 2021; Polcin et al., 2010).

Rural communities in the US report higher rates of substance use and substance use disorders than urban communities (Kelley, 2022). Rural counties have higher opioid prescribing rates and more deaths related to opioid overdoses. Social and environmental factors in rural locations may explain differences in prevalence rates. For example, the normalization of prescription opioid use in rural communities increases use and overdose rates. Isolation, lack of treatment facilities, social and cultural norms, and stigma that may be associated with seeking treatment (such as medication-assisted treatment) are common (Bolinski et al., 2019).

Education and employment are strong predictors of substance use and substance use disorders. Research has found that unemployment is significantly related to substance use and the development of substance use disorders (Henkel, 2011). An emerging body of research indicates that educational attainment, economic conditions, and substance use disorders are related and countercyclical (Kelley, 2022).

Socioeconomic status (SES) impacts substance use and substance use disorder prevalence through lifestyle choices. These choices often explain differences in physical health and psychological health (Wang & Geng, 2019). Individuals with lower SES are more likely to die from alcohol-related deaths than individuals with higher SES. One study found that individuals with low SES were two to five times more likely to die from alcohol-related deaths than individuals with high SES (Probst et al., 2020). This is somewhat surprising since individuals with lower SES report less alcohol consumption than higher SES groups (Lewer et al., 2016). One possible explanation for increased mortality in low SES groups is the addition of other risk factors like obesity, smoking, and other health conditions (Lewer et al., 2016; Probst et al., 2020).

Theories on Substance Use Disorders and Addiction

There are many theories, frameworks, and models used to explain both substance use and addiction in a clinical setting. Many researchers, medical doctors, clinicians, and counselors rely heavily on the bio-psychosocial model to understand and treat addiction. The **biopsychosocial spiritual model** of addiction recognizes that there are multiple factors that either increase or decrease a person's risk for addiction- genetics, biology, mental health, trauma, social norms, and the availability of drugs and alcohol are factored into this model. Similarly, **biopsychosocial spiritual theory** is often used to conceptualize why people use substances, and in some cases become addicted (Figure 2.1).

The **biomedical disease model** relies heavily on the biological reasons related to a disease or illness rather than the spiritual, sociological, or psychological factors. According to this model, an organ (like the brain) experiences a defect (which is caused by something like drug or alcohol consumption) and symptoms of the disease occur (addiction) (Kelley, 2022). Based on the concept that there are genetic and biological factors that contribute to addiction as a brain disease, proponents of the **biomedical disease model** call for cures through abstinence, 12-step models, and medical treatment. One con-

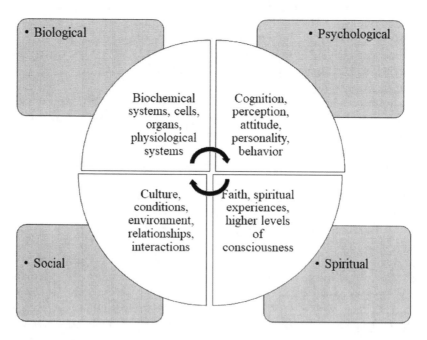

Figure 2.1 Biopsychosocial Spiritual Model.

sideration when calling addiction a disease rather than something else (moral problem, family problem, personality problem, choice), is that by calling it a disease individuals can be treated within a healthcare system, and in most cases, healthcare systems can be reimbursed for the treatment they provide. However, critics of the disease model of addiction feel that it overly pathologizes the brain and the person (Lewis, 2017; Pickard, 2017). Some feel that calling addiction a disease also makes individuals with addiction may feel helpless, disempowered, and dependent on medical providers and clinicians to cure their disease (Pickard, 2017). The **learning model of addiction** explains addiction as the product of learning and development which can be overcome through further learning and development, agency empowerment, self-understanding, and environments that create conditions where these characteristics are developed (Lewis, 2017). Social process theories are also commonly used to explain how to prevent substance use disorders. **Social control theory, behavioral economics, and behavioral choice theory, social learning theory, and stress and coping theory** (Moos, 2007). These four theories are similar because they promote protective social experiences in families, friendship networks, and work relationships. We know that strong bonds with family, friends, school, work, church, and faith-based organizations encourage responsible behaviors, free from drugs, alcohol, or other undesirable behaviors. **Social control theory** tells us that when individuals have weak bonds in any of these areas, they are more likely to drink or engage in unhealthy behaviors. Involvement in protective activities creates a social context that is without drugs, alcohol, or undesirable behaviors. **Behavioral economics or behavioral choice theory** explains that choices and rewards drive decision-making processes. Closely related to **choice theory,** there are five basic needs that humans have and every choice an individual makes is related to these needs. Needs are survival, freedom, fun, power, and love/belonging. Social learning theory unhealthy behaviors like drinking through the lens of role models and social/family contexts. When children or family members witness adults or parents engaging in unhealthy behaviors, they are more likely to engage in these behaviors as well. Bandura's work on social learning theory reminds us that human behaviors are learned by watching how others behave, and that identity, practice, community, and meaning come from learning.

Community and Connection

There is a saying that the opposite of addiction is not recovery, the opposition of addiction is connection. This has been a powerful way to explore and understand what the human spirit needs to overcome and heal. In the 1970s Bruce Alexander conducted a series of rat park experiments to test the power of community, connection, and conditions as they relate to addiction (Gage & Sumnall, 2019). We've used in this our work and teachings as an example of how essential community is in recovery and healing. In these experiments, rats living in parks (highly social environments) were less likely to use morphine than rats living in an isolated environment (without the park). One study found that isolated rats drank more than social rats and females drank more morphine than males (Alexander et al., 1981). Rats living in the park consumed less morphine than rats living in isolation (Alexander et al., 1981). People are not rats, and the rat park model may not be a true representation of the factors that contribute to addiction, but it does point us in a direction of community, connection, health, home, and purpose (Kelley, 2022).

Allyson: How does mastery come into play with alcohol and drug use?
Dee: Mastery ... with alcohol and drug use disorder, the intensity of wanting to taste alcohol or the drugs. So that the physical reaction to it, the physical sensation to it, they can eliminate that feeling. It scares them but it does not overwhelm them. Mastery allows people to not be overwhelmed. If they are overwhelmed they have a skill.

The Spirit of Alcohol and Drugs, Bad Medicine

Alcohol and drugs have spiritual energy. Eduardo Duran writes and talks about this prolifically, and for many individuals struggling with various substance use disorders, it makes sense (Duran, 2006). It resonates. We have to become aware of the energy of alcohol and from that we can begin the process of relating to it in a unique and spiritual manner. It is important that we realize that alcohol spirit energy has awareness and it is this awareness that we are relating to in addiction as well as in recovery.

Eduardo Duran describes addiction as an actual state of possession and a spiritual quest for union with God by real spiritual forces. At the heart of all of this are the intentions individuals have with alcohol, and the reasons why they drink and use drugs. Duran writes about alcohol and drugs as essentially bad medicine, and when consuming drugs and alcohol you are practicing bad medicine against yourself and your family, and your community. His writing and others remind us that our well-being is largely based on our intentions. We have an intention when we drink or use, it is to get high, relaxed, connect, escape, whatever it might be. And what most people do not realize is that alcohol and drugs have a spirit and intentions as well. When we consume these substances and their spirit, we are taking them on, into our own lives, in return, they take something from us. This might be a horrible hangover and feeling bad the next day, or it could even be death from a car crash, or other tragedy that occurs while one is under the influence. Much of depression, anxiety, and substance use is related to loss; the loss of a loved one, the loss of a job, a relationship, or a dream. These losses often result in a spiritual crisis, or crisis of faith. And therefore, grief and loss must be addressed and reckoned with, so that we can endure well, and continue to walk on the healing path.

Moving from abuse to sobriety. Sobriety to self-awareness and abstinence. How do people manage those transition points? It is easy to fall back into our old ways. All of us know that walking, exercising, and not eating fast food are not healthy diets. But look how many fast food places we have, convenience of microwaving, we fall back into patterns easily. How do we have transformative change so that we can see that transformation occur?

Different Populations and Health Paths

We know that access to the healing path is not equal or equitable. And substance use and substance use disorders do not occur equally distributed across populations. Similar to mental health disorders like anxiety and depression mentioned previously, age, gender, race/ethnicity, income, location, and trauma histories influence substance use prevalence. We know that substance use and substance use disorders occur in every race, age, place, and socioeconomic status (Kelley, 2022). The 2018 National Survey on Drug Use and Health reports that American Indian or Alaska Native (AI/AN) populations report the highest rates of substance use disorders, 10.5% AIANs, 9.3% Native Hawaiian or Other Pacific Islander, 7.7% White, 7.1% Hispanic or Latino, 6.9% Black or African American, and 4.8% Asian American (Substance Abuse and Mental Health Services Administration, 2021).

Equity and Equality

Allyson: Can we talk about equity and equality on the healing path? It is missing and this makes it difficult for individuals with substance use disorders or unmet mental health needs to get the services and support they need to heal.

Dee: Yes. When we think about how someone comes into the world- that they come into the world as a gift and we don't say that one person is a better gift than another person. We say that every person is a gift and they are here to learn and grow to become human beings, to develop, to honor their name, to come to know their relatives and recognize them. If we go back to that then everyone should have the same or similar opportunities and access to opportunities and access to resources or needs depending on their circumstances. Equity doesn't mean that everyone gets the same thing. Equity means that everyone has equal opportunity to have access to the same thing. So, that's equal access to food, water, education, protection, safety, to being in families. If we don't provide and support, encourage, and uphold the sacredness of an individual then we are not allowing for the same kind of protection or safety. There was a reason why people were traditionally placed in a circle. If people are in a circle everyone can see one another, every has an opportunity to have a voice. So, there is equity in placement or in having a space and when we think about development and progress being a good relative eliminated some of the harshness of life. There is nothing that is going to be perfect, but if these things are in place for everybody then there is more of an opportunity for equity being felt and exercised better.

We are not in an equitable situation. We're not in a situation where everybody feels included, that the laws are fair or that there are means to have sufficient distribution. And locations create different kinds of demands. So, right now there is a high demand for firefighters, water, and safety when there is a lot of fires going on. There's a high demand for water, relief from the heat, and being able to water plants where there's a drought going on. There is a high demand for negotiation and protection and equal force where there are wars going on. So, we know that there are a lot of things that aren't equal today, that there are a lot of things that are causing demands on human beings. We have a term of recognizing that there is inequality so we talk about social justice and so trying to bring back to this equation that people are sacred beings. That we would treat them in a way that would be helpful for them or to be treated in a way that would be helpful for us.

Allyson: Literature, reports, and books tell us how to different racial and ethnic groups endure well. Rural, urban, LGBTQ, prison populations, juvenile populations, and more. What do we need to know about these unique populations, and enduring well?

Dee: There are various kinds of expertise here. These can come from working with these populations, and different protocols. What you do with populations in rural Alaska compared with urban Baltimore is quite different. But the goal is the same. How do you teach and understand self-regulation? How do you compensate for poverty and oppression, and the injustices when individuals are in different situations, incarcerated, etc., or mental health issues because of white supremacy and colonization? With the Catholic church, all of the priests and nuns sexually abused children. How do you compensate for that or heal from that? IV drug user, poor relationships, how do you bring that information so that someone that is a helper, healer, or mental health provider can have that conversation about past injustices. You can bring understanding or self-awareness, about what caused you to be in this situation, and how can you shift to be in control. Different experts have helped inform our unique understanding and awareness of these issues. Overall, we are talking about self-awareness. The concept is the same, but the practice of how it comes about is different. For example, the practice of flute music. A flute might be very appropriate for someone in a tribal community, but this might not be true for someone from another cultural group. It might be more to do with running, singing, or rap. How do we get that information from all of expertise? Peer mentors, they have the lived experience of these things … . this requires an understanding, flexible boundaries, and transitions.

Self-Regulation and Self-Awareness: Practical Applications

Allyson: What about self-regulation, self-awareness, and addiction. These seem to be the overarching themes that show up when we are talking about enduring well. What does this look like in the real world?

Dee: You must have the awareness of what is going on, what is wrong, before you move on to regulating those behaviors. How people do this and what they call it might be different. In some ways, we do this in our work. We tell people who are using substances not to hang around their old friends. We don't help them to figure out how to manage in those tricky situations when they are with their old friends, we fall back into those patterns. People have their favorite coffee cup no matter how stained it is, you wear a certain jersey when you watch your football team play, you sit in the same chair every day when you read the paper. With mental health, trauma, and substance abuse we have these rituals that we also work with that we institute. For some people, smells and sounds are big trigger. So, self-awareness is a big trigger.

Allyson: What about medication as treatment?

Dee: You can take medication for anxiety, depression, or addiction. How do we assess what is medically needed to have this shift? How do we view mental health, and do we feel like it is a failure of self will? In terms of having anxiety attacks, struggling with depression. There are some genetic factors that can come into play. Being able to have various kinds of support and protocols that may include medication can help people. This depends on what individuals deem as necessary and helpful. Some people because of their level of depression, they do shock treatments. Most of us in the general population or profession would say oh my goodness, shock treatment, which is pretty severe. That is not anything that I would view as acceptable. But people who are severely depressed find this treatment extremely helpful. They engage in it with a schedule.

How we think about what is helpful has to be individually assessed. Somebody with severe depression may have self-awareness and self-regulation but they still may need shock treatment. Someone with anxiety may do all of the grounding practices, but may still have high anxiety, but would manage to suffer through it. Not because they recognize that they can act. It is just that they have such high anxiety, and they self-medicate with prescription, alcohol, or other drugs. People may see their anxiety as debilitating, but they are able to manage it, but not well. Because it is so overwhelming.

Allyson: To know that the process of healing is really about finding out what works for you, as an individual, based on your self-awareness of what you need. And, to recognize the patterns (physical, mental, thinking) that get us into a place of being pitiful, and knowing what we need to continue on a healing path. A few years ago you wrote a booklet for Eastern Shoshone Recovery on self-regulation and ceremony.

Dee: Yes. Me and my son, Ah-in-ist Sipes wrote this, Ceremony Teaches Self-Regulation. Here are some messages about ceremony that can help people with depression, anxiety, substance use, and feeling unwell.

Ceremony has many components. Essential to ceremony is the spiritual guidance that comes from that Great Mystery. We did not address that Great Mystery except to say it exists and that ceremony would not be meaningful without it. An acknowledgment of that Great Mystery is important.

As a background to ceremonial ways, there are underlying beliefs that guide instruction. There is an eternal belief among the Indigenous Peoples of this Great Turtle Island that each walks a sacred path occupied by both spirit and reasoning. That there is a purpose for this journey. That there is order and structure to the beginning of human beings, and a need for understanding "where we come from, why we are here, and where we are going." There is recognition that individuals do not walk this path alone and there are many relatives who walk together. Families and relatives are essential features of this sacred path.

It is important to understand that ceremonies do not function like a numeral equation or chemical mixture. The act of a ceremony in itself cannot bring the desired result without the personal preparation they require and following self-reflection in the days and seasons that follow.

It has been taught that all ceremonies were given to us by the Creator and Spirits to be used only to benefit the people as the Creator and Sprits directed and as the People requested. This sacred knowledge that is used to perform ceremony by Holy People and gained by the individuals or families participating is never be used as a tool of manipulation, self-aggrandizement, or punishment but only to uplift, to connect, and reestablish one's natural place in the Land, Earth, and Universe.

Ceremony is not an observable event unless you are being instructed since ceremony is participatory. Ceremony is not entertainment, rather is the process of learning who you are, the process of self-discovery, self-regulation, and sacrifice. Of course, there are many kinds of ceremonies within the cultures of the American Indian. Our intent was to explain how self-regulation occurs within the process of participating in ceremony. A great gain is created when one can bring emotional, relational, physical, and spiritual regulation into how one functions as a human being.

Ceremony can be a simple gesture of making an offering of tobacco or of water. It can involve one person or hundreds. It can be led by a male and/or a female, even by a child or an elder of many years. As a participant, attentiveness and openness are important attributes to embrace as one learns self-regulation. Instruction can be one-time instruction but typically is a series of repetitions in order to evolve into self-awareness and practice. Once instruction is given, then a single individual may consider to engage in ceremony alone. For example, daily prayer is ceremony. There can be significant differences between ritual and ceremony, however, at times they may be the same. Rituals can occur out of heightened anxiety and/or without understanding purpose, i.e., throwing salt over your shoulder or putting a tooth under your pillow. There may be a repetition of rituals that may feel compulsive and unproductive. Ceremony should be purposeful and have meaning with active engagement of mind, body, and spirit.

Ceremony is about preparation, sacrifice, service, reflection, offerings, and grounding that results in self-regulation. The definition of self-regulation involves controlling one's behavior, emotions, and thoughts in the pursuit of short-term and long-term outcomes. More specifically, emotional self-regulation refers to the ability to manage disruptive emotions (feelings), behavioral impulses and actions (doing), and intrusive or negative thoughts (thinking). Self-regulation is an ongoing process that is practice daily and improved over time. For ceremony, there is a preparation which includes planning, scheduling, and thoughtful engagement with ceremonial individuals and family or others that guide actions. One instruction that is typically given is to think good thoughts in preparation for moving toward ceremony. Sacrifice is a significant aspect of ceremony, not only in preparation but in the actual ceremony. It is common to refrain from food and water for a specific period of time; this can also include refraining from negative thinking, giving up bad habits that might be harmful long term (alcohol), and eliminating some comforts such as sleeping in a bed vs sleeping on the ground. Service can be broad and general or narrow and specific. For example, digging fire pits or taking on a long-term commitment to take food to elders or offer transportation. Reflection is the effort to be self-aware and accepting feedback and instruction without being offended or reactionary. Humility is a gift that is accepted in order for self-regulation to become more integrated and solidified. Offerings have variety and require preparation if they are not readily available and can be as diverse as cultural teachings that drive gift-giving. Offering and sacrifice can be overlapping from an organic origin to creating offerings such as star quilts to gathering and tying sage bundles. Generosity has also been part of offerings and demonstrates the desire to share blessings with others. This is a very purposeful action on the part of the person and their support group moving toward a specific ceremony. Grounding is an old concept that is critical to knowing "who you are" and "where you are going." Song, drumming, smudging, prayer, touch, water, food, words, or other physical or spiritual means can help with the grounding. Self-regulation is drawing from all these aspects to increase how to think, feel, and do.

What Now?

We outlined what depression, anxiety, and substance use look like in our world. We explained research, theories, and approaches used in understanding these issues and how they impact our ability to walk on a healing path. And we recognize that some of the major barriers that get in the way of enduring well or walking on the healing path are unresolved trauma, violence, poverty, oppression, and historical trauma. We presented concepts of ceremony as self-regulation and how purposeful actions and intentions help us on the healing path.

Resources

Anxiety

Stanley J. Rachman, Routledge 2020 Rachman's in depth review of anxiety outlines the nature of anxiety, theories related to anxiety, related anxiety disorders, and treatment approaches. Available at: https://www.routledge.com/Anxiety/Rachman-Rachman/p/book/9781138311299?utm_source=cjaffiliates&utm_medium=affiliates&cjevent=94939a0d126511ed81869f160a1c0e14

Depression: The Facts

Danuta Wasserman, Oxford University Press 2011, This comprehensive book explains the symptoms of depression, causes of depression, and treatment of depression. Available at: https://www.amazon.com/Depression-Facts-Danuta-Wasserman/dp/019960293X

Depression

National Institutes of Mental Health, 2022, This website resource summarizes what depression is, signs and symptoms, risk factors, treatments, and therapies, and current studies on depression. https://www.nimh.nih.gov/health/topics/depression# :~:text=Depression%20is%20one%20of%20the%20most%20common%20mental,at %20any%20age%2C%20but%20often%20begins%20in%20adulthood.

Spirituality, Religion, and Mental Health, David Rosamrin and Harold Koenig, Academic Press, 2020, This book provides a comprehensive overview of spirituality and relationship as it relates to mental health, addiction, disease, and other health topics. Authors link empirical evidence, ethical considerations, and clinical issues into each chapter. Available at: https://www.amazon.com/Handbook-Religion-Mental-Health-Rosmarin

Suicide Data and Statistics

Centers for Disease Control and Prevention, 2022, This website includes the prevalence of suicide, populations at greater risk and resources available. https://www.cdc.gov/ suicide/suicide-data-statistics.html

Substance Use and Mental Health Indicators

Substance Abuse and Mental Health Services Administration, 2020, This report provides national data on substance use and mental health indicators, outlining prevalence, demographic differences, and comparisons from previous years. https://www. samhsa.gov/data/sites/default/files/reports/rpt35325/NSDUHFFRPDFWHT-MLFiles2020/2020NSDUHFFR1PDFW102121.pdf

Healing the Soul Wound

Eduardo Duran, Teachers College Press 2019, This book reviews literature, stresses cultural competence, and connection, and addresses treatment from the perspective of spirit/soul wound and healing. Chapter 5 focuses on the spirit of alcohol and training addiction. Available from: https://www.amazon.com/Healing-Soul-Wound-Trauma-Informed-Multicultural/dp/0807761397?asin=B081D9LQCV& revisionId=38bcf9bd&format=1&depth=1

The Brain and Drugs

National Institutes on Drug Addiction, 2020, This report provides a comprehensive summary of drugs and the brain, risk and protective factors, and why some people experience addiction while others do not. https://nida.nih.gov/publications/drugs-brains-behavior-science-addiction/drugs-brain

References

Aldridge, R. W., Story, A., Hwang, S. W., Nordentoft, M., Luchenski, S. A., Hartwell, G., Tweed, E. J., Lewer, D., Vittal Katikireddi, S., & Hayward, A. C. (2018). Morbidity and mortality in homeless individuals, prisoners, sex workers, and individuals with substance use disorders in high-income countries: A systematic review and meta-analysis. *Lancet (London, England)*, *391*(10117), 241–250. https://doi.org/10.1016/S0140-6736(17)31869-X

Alexander, B. K., Beyerstein, B. L., Hadaway, P. F., & Coambs, R. B. (1981). Effect of early and later colony housing on oral ingestion of morphine in rats. *Pharmacology Biochemistry and Behavior*, *15*(4), 571–576. https://doi.org/10.1016/0091-3057(81)90211-2

American Psyhological Association. (2020). *APA Guidelines for Psychological Assessment and Evaluation: (510142020-001)* [Data set]. American Psychological Association. https://doi.org/10.1037/e510142020-001

Austin, A. E., Shiue, K. Y., Naumann, R. B., Figgatt, M. C., Gest, C., & Shanahan, M. E. (2021). Associations of housing stress with later substance use outcomes: A systematic review. *Addictive Behaviors*, *123*, 107076. https://doi.org/10.1016/j.addbeh.2021.107076

Beck, A. T., & Beck, A. T. (1979). *Cognitive therapy of depression*. Guilford Press; WorldCat.org. http://www.gbv.de/dms/bowker/toc/9780898629194.pdf

Bolinski, R., Ellis, K., Zahnd, W. E., Walters, S., McLuckie, C., Schneider, J., Rodriguez, C., Ezell, J., Friedman, S. R., Pho, M., & Jenkins, W. D. (2019). Social norms associated with nonmedical opioid use in rural communities: A systematic review. *Translational Behavioral Medicine*, *9*(6), 1224–1232. https://doi.org/10.1093/tbm/ibz129

Bueno-Notivol, J., Gracia-García, P., Olaya, B., Lasheras, I., López-Antón, R., & Santabárbara, J. (2021). Prevalence of depression during the COVID-19 outbreak: A meta-analysis of community-based studies. *International Journal of Clinical and Health Psychology*, *21*(1), 100196. https://doi.org/10.1016/j.ijchp.2020.07.007

COVID-19 Mental Disorders Collaborators. (2021). Global prevalence and burden of depressive and anxiety disorders in 204 countries and territories in 2020 due to the COVID-19 pandemic. *Lancet (London, England)*, *398*(10312), 1700–1712. https://doi.org/10.1016/S0140-6736(21)02143-7

Dennis, M., Babor, T. F., Roebuck, M. C., & Donaldson, J. (2002). Changing the focus: The case for recognizing and treating cannabis use disorders. *Addiction (Abingdon, England)*, *97*(Suppl 1), 4–15. https://doi.org/10.1046/j.1360-0443.97.s01.10.x

Domschke, K., & Maron, E. (2013). Genetic factors in anxiety disorders. *Modern Trends in Pharmacopsychiatry*, *29*, 24–46. https://doi.org/10.1159/000351932

Duran, E. 1949-. (2006). *Healing the soul wound: Counseling with American Indians and other native peoples*. Teachers College Press; WorldCat.org. http://catdir.loc.gov/catdir/toc/fy0609/2005046666.html

Escohotado, A. (1999). *A brief history of drugs: From the Stone Age to the Stoned Age*. Park Street Press.

Funk, R. R., McDermeit, M., Godley, S. H., & Adams, L. (2003). Maltreatment issues by level of adolescent substance abuse treatment: The extent of the problem at intake and relationship to early outcomes. *Child Maltreatment*, *8*(1), 36–45. https://doi.org/10.1177/1077559502239607

Gage, S. H., & Sumnall, H. R. (2019). Rat Park: How a rat paradise changed the narrative of addiction. *Addiction*, *114*(5), 917–922. https://doi.org/10.1111/add.14481

Gilbert, P. A., Pass, L. E., Keuroghlian, A. S., Greenfield, T. K., & Reisner, S. L. (2018). Alcohol research with transgender populations: A systematic review and recommendations to strengthen future studies. *Drug and Alcohol Dependence, 186*, 138–146. https://doi.org/10.1016/j.drugalcdep.2018.01.016

Goodwin, R. D., Weinberger, A. H., Kim, J. H., Wu, M., & Galea, S. (2020). Trends in anxiety among adults in the United States, 2008–2018: Rapid increases among young adults. *Journal of Psychiatric Research, 130*, 441–446. https://doi.org/10.1016/j.jpsychires.2020.08.014

Grant, B. F., Goldstein, R. B., Saha, T. D., Chou, S. P., Jung, J., Zhang, H., Pickering, R. P., Ruan, W. J., Smith, S. M., Huang, B., & Hasin, D. S. (2015). Epidemiology of DSM-5 alcohol use disorder: Results from the National Epidemiologic Survey on Alcohol and Related Conditions III. *JAMA Psychiatry, 72*(8), 757–766. https://doi.org/10.1001/jamapsychiatry.2015.0584

Henkel, D. (2011). Unemployment and substance use: A review of the literature (1990–2010). *Current Drug Abuse Reviews, 4*(1), 4–27. https://doi.org/10.2174/1874473711104010004

Kaufman, J. A., Salas-Hernández, L. K., Komro, K. A., & Livingston, M. D. (2020). Effects of increased minimum wages by unemployment rate on suicide in the USA. *Journal of Epidemiology and Community Health, 74*(3), 219–224. https://doi.org/10.1136/jech-2019-212981

Kelley, A. (2022). *Treatment program evaluation: Public health perspectives on mental health and substance use disorders* (Vol. 1–1 online resource). Routledge; WorldCat.org. https://doi.org/0.4324/9781003290728

Kelley, A., BigFoot, D., Small, C., Mexicancheyenne, T., & Gondara, R. (2015). Recommendations from an American Indian reservation community-based suicide prevention program. *International Journal of Human Rights in Healthcare, 8*(1), 3–13. https://doi.org/10.1108/IJHRH-10-2013-0025

Kelley, A., Restad, D., & Killsback, J. (2018). A public health approach: Documenting the risk and protective factors of suicide ideation in one American Indian community. *Psychological Services, 15*(3), 325–331. https://doi.org/10.1037/ser0000211

Khoury, L., Tang, Y. L., Bradley, B., Cubells, J. F., & Ressler, K. J. (2010). Substance use, childhood traumatic experience, and posttraumatic stress disorder in an urban civilian population. *Depression and Anxiety, 27*(12), 1077–1086. https://doi.org/10.1002/da.20751

Kircanski, K., LeMoult, J., Ordaz, S., & Gotlib, I. H. (2017). Investigating the nature of co-occurring depression and anxiety: Comparing diagnostic and dimensional research approaches. *Journal of Affective Disorders, 216*, 123–135. https://doi.org/10.1016/j.jad.2016.08.006

Kushner, M. G., Krueger, R., Frye, B., & Peterson, J. (2008). Epidemiological perspectives on co-occurring anxiety disorder and substance use disorder. In S. H. Stewart & P. J. Conrod (Eds.), *Anxiety and substance use disorders: The vicious cycle of comorbidity* (pp. 3–17). Springer US. https://doi.org/10.1007/978-0-387-74290-8_1

Lewer, D., Meier, P., Beard, E., Boniface, S., & Kaner, E. (2016). Unravelling the alcohol harm paradox: A population-based study of social gradients across very heavy drinking thresholds. *BMC Public Health, 16*, 599. https://doi.org/10.1186/s12889-016-3265-9

Lewis, M. (2017). Addiction and the brain: Development, not disease. *Neuroethics*, *10*(1), 7–18. https://doi.org/10.1007/s12152-016-9293-4

Martin, C. S., Sher, K. J., & Chung, T. (2011). Hazardous use should not be a diagnostic criterion for substance use disorders in DSM-5. *Journal of Studies on Alcohol and Drugs*, *72*, 685–686. 10.15288/jsad.2011.72.685

Masterson, K. (2010, February 10). "Cutting" Elevated From Symptom To Mental Disorder. *NPR*. https://www.npr.org/2010/02/10/123529829/cutting-elevated-from-symptom-to-mental-disorder

Maté, G. (2008). *In the realm of hungry ghosts: Close encounters with addiction*. Random House Digital, Inc.

McLellan, A. (2017). Substance misuse and substance use disorders: Why do they matter in healthcare? *Transactions of the American Clinical and Climatological Association*, *128*, 112–130. https://www.ncbi.nlm.nih.gov/pmc/articles/PMC5525418/

Millard, C. (2015). *A history of self-harm in Britain*. Palgrave Macmillan Wellcome Trust. https://doi.org/10.1057/9781137529626

Moos, R. H. (2007). Theory-based active ingredients of effective treatments for substance use disorders. *Drug and Alcohol Dependence*, *88*(2–3), 109–121. https://doi.org/10.1016/j.drugalcdep.2006.10.010

National Institutes of Mental Health. (2022). *Depression*. National Institute of Mental Health (NIMH). https://www.nimh.nih.gov/health/topics/depression

Nielsen, IQ. (2020). Rebalancing the 'Covid-19 Effect' on Alcohol Sales [Online]. Available: https://www.nielsen.com/us/en/insights/article/2020/rebalancing-the-covid-19-effect-on-alcohol-sales/. [Accessed on 12.09.2020].

Pickard, H. (2017). Responsibility without blame for addiction. *Neuroethics*, *10*(1), 169–180. https://doi.org/10.1007/s12152-016-9295-2

Polcin, D. L., Korcha, R. A., Bond, J., & Galloway, G. (2010). Sober living houses for alcohol and drug dependence: 18-Month outcomes. *Journal of Substance Abuse Treatment*, *38*(4), 356–365. https://doi.org/10.1016/j.jsat.2010.02.003

Probst, C., Kilian, C., Sanchez, S., Lange, S., & Rehm, J. (2020). The role of alcohol use and drinking patterns in socioeconomic inequalities in mortality: A systematic review. *The Lancet Public Health*, *5*(6), e324–e332. https://doi.org/10.1016/S2468-2667(20)30052-9

Rachman, S. J. (2019). *Anxiety* (4th ed.). Psychology Press. https://doi.org/10.4324/9780429458958

Racine, N., McArthur, B. A., Cooke, J. E., Eirich, R., Zhu, J., & Madigan, S. (2021). Global prevalence of depressive and anxiety symptoms in children and adolescents during COVID-19: A meta-analysis. *JAMA Pediatrics*, *175*(11), 1142–1150. https://doi.org/10.1001/jamapediatrics.2021.2482

Ramchand, R., Gordon, J. A., & Pearson, J. L. (2021). Trends in suicide rates by race and ethnicity in the United States. *JAMA Network Open*, *4*(5), e2111563. https://doi.org/10.1001/jamanetworkopen.2021.11563

Ribeiro, J. D., & Joiner, T. E. (2009). The interpersonal-psychological theory of suicidal behavior: Current status and future directions. *Journal of Clinical Psychology*, *65*(12), 1291–1299. https://doi.org/10.1002/jclp.20621

Richmond-Rakerd, L. S., Slutske, W. S., & Wood, P. K. (2017). Age of initiation and substance use progression: A multivariate latent growth analysis. *Psychology of Addictive*

Behaviors: Journal of the Society of Psychologists in Addictive Behaviors, 31(6), 664–675. https://doi.org/10.1037/adb0000304

Ritchie, H., & Roser, M. (2018). Mental health. *Our World in Data.* https://ourworldindata.org/mental-health

Roberts, A., Rogers, J., Mason, R., Siriwardena, A. N., Hogue, T., Whitley, G. A., & Law, G. R. (2021). Alcohol and other substance use during the COVID-19 pandemic: A systematic review. *Drug and Alcohol Dependence, 229,* 109150. https://doi.org/10.1016/j.drugalcdep.2021.109150

Schick, M. R., Spillane, N. S., & Hostetler, K. L. (2020). A call to action: A systematic review examining the failure to include females and members of minoritized racial/ethnic groups in clinical trials of pharmacological treatments for alcohol use disorder. *Alcoholism: Clinical and Experimental Research, 44*(10), 1933–1951. https://doi.org/10.1111/acer.14440

Schuler, M. S., Rice, C. E., Evans-Polce, R. J., & Collins, R. (2018). Disparities in substance use behaviors and disorders among adult sexual minorities by age, gender, and sexual identity. *Drug and Alcohol Dependence, 189,* 139–146. https://doi.org/10.1016/j.drugalcdep.2018.05.008

Siris, S. G. (2001). Suicide and schizophrenia. *Journal of Psychopharmacology, 15*(2), 127–135. https://doi.org/10.1177/026988110101500209

Smith, J. P., & Book, S. W. (2008). Anxiety and substance use disorders: A review. *The Psychiatric Times, 25*(10), 19–23. https://www.ncbi.nlm.nih.gov/pmc/articles/PMC2904966/

Stack, S. (2021). Contributing factors to suicide: Political, social, cultural and economic. *Preventive Medicine, 152*(Pt1), 106498. https://doi.org/10.1016/j.ypmed.2021.106498

Stanis, J. J., & Andersen, S. L. (2014). Reducing substance use during adolescence: A translational framework for prevention. *Psychopharmacology, 231*(8), 1437–1453. https://doi.org/10.1007/s00213-013-3393-1

Substance Abuse and Mental Health Services Administration. (2021). *2020 National Survey of Drug Use and Health (NSDUH) Releases | CBHSQ Data.* https://www.samhsa.gov/data/release/2020-national-survey-drug-use-and-health-nsduh-releases

Volkow, N. D., Poznyak, V., Saxena, S., & Gerra, G. (2017). Drug use disorders: Impact of a public health rather than a criminal justice approach. *World Psychiatry, 16*(2), 213–214. https://doi.org/10.1002/wps.20428

Wang, J., & Geng, L. (2019). Effects of socioeconomic status on physical and psychological health: Lifestyle as a mediator. *International Journal of Environmental Research and Public Health, 16*(2), 281. https://doi.org/10.3390/ijerph16020281

Wasserman, D. (2011). *Depression.* Oxford University Press USA - OSO. http://ebookcentral.proquest.com/lib/uncg/detail.action?docID=975635

World Health Organization (WHO). (2019). Suicide Worldwide in 2019. Global Health Estimates. Available from: https://www.who.int/publications/i/item/9789240026643

Zapolski, T. C. B., Pedersen, S. L., McCarthy, D. M., & Smith, G. T. (2014). Less drinking, yet more problems: Understanding African American drinking and related problems. *Psychological Bulletin, 140*(1), 188–223. https://doi.org/10.1037/a0032113

Chapter 3

Trauma

Trauma

The butterfly is proof that you can go through a great deal of darkness and become something beautiful.

Trauma is not a new phenomenon. There has always been trauma, in every generation, in ever century of mankind. There are various kinds of traumas, i.e., collective trauma, cumulative trauma, natural disasters, man-made traumatic events, displacement, losses, injuries, failures, and death. The only unique thing about trauma is that each person experiences trauma individually and personally even when the event affects thousands or millions such as wars, plagues or famine. Not everyone responds in the same way when they experience a traumatic event but there are human responses involving the cognitive, emotional, physical, spiritual, and relational elements that because of being human are similar. Fear, confusion, loss of control, hypervigilance, sense of danger and perceptions of threats, shame, anger, and other negative thoughts and feelings undermine safety, protection, security, predictability, and stability resulting in brokenness.

Dee: In Oklahoma, there are frequent tornados, in fact, it is called tornado alley because tornadoes tend to follow a common path that devastates sections of certain towns that are in that tornado alley path. Some people move, while other families see themselves as being highly resilient and committed to their communities, they rebuild and rebuild. Others find that level of threat too menacing to experience each spring when tornado seasons arrives. Same event but different outcomes. When there is a significant group of people who have experienced the same thing, they may have similar responses. At the same time when two siblings experience the death of a parent, they may not react in the same way.

Everyone experiences trauma, but everyone has different responses.

DOI: 10.4324/9781003274018-3

Trauma can be defined as an extreme or upsetting experience that prevents an individual from functioning in their current situation. Traumatic events that occur in our lives may be acute or chronic or collective.

Acute Traumatic Events

- Disaster
- Suicide
- Homicide
- Accidents
- Sudden, unexpected, violent loss or death

Chronic Traumatic Events

- Death
- Illness
- Abuse
- Neglect
- Sudden, unexpected, violent loss or death

Collective trauma involves psychological reactions to events that affect an entire society or community (Hirschberger, 2018). Collective trauma is different from acute or chronic trauma because it is deeply embedded in our memories, which causes us to relive and remember the traumas, even if we were not present. Examples of collective trauma include colonization, the Holocaust, school shootings, and the 9/11 terrorist attacks.

Historical trauma includes the experiences of emotional and psychological wounding in an individual. Genocide and forced assimilation / colonization are examples of historical trauma experienced by American Indian/Alaska Native populations (AI/ANs). AI/ANs experience the highest number and variety of Adverse Childhood Experiences (ACEs), the highest rates of physical abuse, sexual abuse, parental substance abuse, and witnessing violence than persons from any other racial/ethnic group (Richards et al., 2021). **Intergenerational trauma** is historical trauma that spans multiple generations and affects communities and their descendants (Pumariega et al., 2022).

Dee: Prior to colonization, American Indian and Alaska Native families were strong, interdependent, and balanced. Families believed that each member was part of the Sacred Circle and children were the center of the Circle. Each member came from that Circle and to care for one another was an important duty and obligation for all members. Social roles were filled based on tribal protocols and practices. When individual members of a tribe or community did not fill their role, or violated a traditional law or protocol, they would be punished according to tribal / community laws. These laws were enforced and understood because they originated in the community. The US government undermined the structure of traditional laws and community control through boarding schools, missions, treaties, forced removal from ancestral lands, and various forms of abuse, oppression, and violence. These actions impacted every facet of life for American Indian and Alaska Native families; their unity, stability, and ability to govern themselves was taken away. Boarding schools were perhaps the most devastating to families and communities since they changed the traditional family environment, reducing familial and communal interdependence. As a result of boarding schools and the loss of family functioning, many children learned unhealthy behaviors and experienced physical and sexual abuse. Historical and generational trauma resulting from the boarding school era is evident in tribal communities and families today. Linked to this history is the current crisis of diminished faith and spirituality among many American Indian and Alaska Native people. With a history of traumas and violence, priests, nuns, and other spiritual leaders have been convicted of sexual abuse, resulting in wide-spread distrust of religious establishments throughout the United States. In one case involving hundreds of American Indians and Alaska Natives, the attorney for the abuse victims reported that it wasn't an accident, the evidence showed the church did it on purpose and it was rape.

Allyson: This is definitely trauma that shows up in our work and is especially important for understanding trauma and healing from sexual abuse.

Understanding Trauma

There are different ways that we come to understand what trauma means. The American Psychological Association defines a traumatic event as something that an individual experiences, witnesses, or has been confronted with. These events may be something that has actually occurred, or they could be threats to death, injury, or sexual violence (DeAngelis, 2013). The Substance Abuse and Mental Health Services Administration describes trauma as an event or circumstance that results in physical, emotional, and or life threatening harm. The National Traumatic Stress Network created definitions of trauma that individuals may experience (After Trauma Empowerment Network, 2022; National Child Traumatic Stress Network, 2022).

• Sexual Abuse or Assault: Actual or attempted sexual contact, exposure to age-inappropriate sexual material or environments, sexual exploitation, unwanted or coercive sexual contact. Includes sexual human trafficking and exploitation.

- Physical Abuse or Assault: Actual or attempted infliction of physical pain with or without use of an object or weapon and including use of severe corporal punishment.
- Emotional Abuse/Psychological Maltreatment: Acts of commission against a child or adult, other than physical or sexual abuse, that caused or could have caused conduct, cognitive, affective or other mental disturbance, such as verbal abuse, emotional abuse, excessive demands on a person's performance that may lead to negative self-image and disturbing behavior. Acts of omission against a child that caused or could have caused conduct, cognitive, affective or other mental disturbance, such as emotional neglect or intentional social deprivation.
- Neglect: Failure by the child victim's caretaker(s) to provide needed, age-appropriate care although financially able to do so, or offered financial or other means to do so, including physical neglect, medical neglect, or educational neglect.
- Serious Accident or Illness/Medical Procedure: Unintentional injury or accident, having a physical illness or experiencing medical procedures that are extremely painful and/or life-threatening.
- Witness to Domestic Violence: Exposure to emotional abuse, actual/attempted physical or sexual assault, or aggressive control perpetrated between a parent/caretaker and another adult in the child victim's home environment or perpetrated by an adolescent against one or more adults in the child victim's home environment.
- Victim/Witness to Community Violence: Extreme violence in the community, including exposure to gang-related violence.
- School Violence: Violence that occurs in a school setting, including, but not limited to school shootings, bullying, interpersonal violence among classmates, and classmate suicide.
- Natural or Manmade Disasters: Major accident or disaster that is an unintentional result of a manmade or natural event.
- Forced Displacement: Forced relocation to a new home due to political reasons, generally including political asylees or immigrants fleeing political persecution.
- War/Terrorism/Political Violence: Exposure to acts of war/terrorism/political violence including incidents such bombing, shooting, looting, or accidents that are a result of terrorist activity as well as actions of individuals acting in isolation if they are considered political in nature.
- Victim/Witness to Extreme Personal/Interpersonal Violence: Includes extreme violence by or between individuals including exposure to homicide, suicide and other similar extreme events.
- Traumatic Grief/Separation: Death of a parent, primary caretaker or sibling, abrupt and/or unexpected, accidental or premature death or homicide of a close friend, family member, or other close relative; abrupt,

unexplained and/or indefinite separation from a parent, primary caretaker or sibling due to circumstances beyond the child victim's control.

- System-Induced Trauma: Traumatic removal from the home, traumatic foster placement, sibling separation, or multiple placements in a short amount of time.
- Intergenerational Trauma: The transmission of trauma from one generation to the next.

Allyson: We know from research that violence, poverty, historical trauma, and oppression create traumatic conditions and responses. Trauma exposure may create personal imbalance and manifest in unhealthy behaviors and attitudes. Traumatic stressors (that is stress caused by a traumatic event) make people vulnerable and at risk for mental health and substance use disorders. When a traumatic event occurs, the healing path is disrupted. When trauma is not adequately addressed it is difficult to walk on a healing path. Individuals often feel imbalanced, broken, and not walking in the direction that they want to go.

Dee: When animals are hurt in the wild, they seek safety and support to heal. Animals may not know how to adapt to unexpected changes in their environment or their lives. Some animals have not been able to adapt so people have helped them. Once animals recover from their injury, they are ready to return to the wild, to their circle of life. In the same way, humans often need help adapting to unexpected changes in their lives. To heal from trauma, humans need the strength and support of others. This might be family members, friends, their community, church, and other healers and helpers (BigFoot & Schmidt, 2022).

Support networks, resources, history, faith, spirituality, dispositions, environment, self-affirmations, are all part of the healing from trauma process. But much of our healing depends on how much we reach out for help when we need it, and the help that we offer others when they are in need. When families have family members die by suicide, some reach out immediately if they hear about someone wanting to harm themselves, even in their own pain they can reach out. They try to alleviate the suffering of others.

Allyson: Suicide is a traumatic event for families. And individuals who died by suicide have often experienced trauma that is unresolved. Why do some people survive these traumatic events, and others do not see a way out, they take their own lives?

Dee: I think it is a story of endurance. My daughter experienced a very traumatic event. She is the most spiritual being that I know. She has unwavering faith. She has endured well. My son did not endure well.

He was the victim of sexual abuse, self-loathing, pain, agony, hurt, sorrow. He kept making decisions that caused him more self-harm. He died because of self-harm. Should I judge him, that he did not endure well? My daughter sends postcards to our elderly church sisters, because of COVID they don't go to church. The sister leadership in our congregation asked her if she would write a card. She graciously agreed. This has helped her endure well. She has an unwavering faith. She has taught me that we can grow from our burdens. When bad things happen, when trauma happens do we blame others? Do we blame those who have caused harm? Do we blame ourselves? I did for a while. But there is a bottomless pit of sorrow ... we cannot go there.

Trauma is inevitable but it does not have to be devastating continuously. It is devastating in the moment. Gratitude. Grace. Generosity. Service. These attributes help with the traumatic impact.

Spirit is at the center of our response to traumatic events. Everything has to be working in connection and balance to the other parts of our being (Figure 3.1).

- Relational (sense of belonging, connection, and support within our relationships)
- Thinking, mental, cognitive, intellect (work, community, processing)
- Affect, emotional, feelings, emotions (wellbeing, ability to manage and self-regulate, meaning and purpose)
- Behavior, physical body, gender (reactions, movement, roles)

Figure 3.1 Spirit at the Center.

Allyson: I find myself avoiding certain situations, conflicts, and people. I know that avoidance is probably not one of the characteristics of the healing path, but sometimes we just have to survive.

Dee: Well, I think that it's a common human attribute or trait that we don't want to deal with things that are unpleasant or feel just uncomfortable about or confused. That's not an unusual thing. When we get embarrassed, when we get fearful, when we have those emotions that make us uncomfortable in some way or distressed or depressed it's natural. It's a natural, natural, natural thing to practice avoidance. The question is does this impact your quality of life because of avoidance a place, person, event, words, or feelings?

Allyson: That reminds me of the story of the buffalo.

Dee: Yes. There's a story told by the elders. One of the things that the buffalo taught us is they knew how to protect their little ones. The buffalo circle around the little ones to protect them, this is to freeze. Or in some cases, they turn around and run toward a threat that is a fight. Or sometimes they run from it. They flee. That is the body's response, physically to trauma. The response is to either freeze, fight or flee. And so, when we think about the natural response of avoidance, it is really fleeing from it. And also, the natural response is to fight, also a natural response is to freeze, sometimes in quick succession and very quickly over and over. An individual or a group can do all of those things all at once within a relatively short period of time, somebody could start to walk away turn around and come back and start yelling and get so that they couldn't even say anything and freeze up and that can help happen within a three or four second span, all three of those things. And sometimes they can extend it so that they're always running, or they're always freezing, or they're always fighting. Suddenly, you're just sitting there and now you started fighting and get so aggressive/hostile, that it feels impossible to calm down.

Animals have always been our teachers. They teach us when to stay and fight, to run, to fly to form a circle, to become a herd, or to escape danger. We have to be aware of what we see, think, feel, and how we respond. By understanding our body's reaction to a situation, we can understand that it's the spirit's way of telling us how to care for ourselves in a new way.

Allyson: Our environment and surroundings play such a critical role in how we respond to trauma, and how we endure well. Our comfort level. Our ability to trust. Feel. Self-regulate. Stay calm. So how do we walk on a healing path and have those critical conversations, while staying safe?

Dee: When we think about it in that way, not wanting to talk about things that are unpleasant, it's a way of coping that is part of our natural, biological, genetic, survival, mechanisms and so how do we make an environment safe enough that those conversations can occur? How do we make the environment or the surroundings safe enough to have dialogue, when people have the sense to flee, fight or freeze and not be able to have the kind of responses they want? So, I think what we have to think about is that environment. How safe is a place that encourages this kind of hard dialogue? Even when people don't want to talk about things, you can still create a safe environment. And it could be gradual. So, we talked about gradual exposure being able to allow people a little bit, a little bit, a little bit, you know until there's a bigger opportunity. And so gradual exposure is the old technique. When you think about a sweat lodge, a sweat lodge uses gradual exposure. So, they start with the first round and a few rocks and they add more rocks and more and more rocks with each round until they use up all the rocks. And so gradual exposure is not a new understanding. It's an old practice that we are now applying in a lot of therapeutic settings, but it's something we do all the time. You do it with driving. You do it with people learning a new skill. You go out there and you practice a little bit and you get better and you practice a little bit more and you get better and you practice a little bit more building confidence and improved self-esteem. People don't always think of it in terms of therapeutic environments that can be supported in order to have these difficult conversations.

There are many people who want to get it over with. They think, let's face this head-on and get it over with and done with so I don't have to deal with it again. In many ways, it is a fight response but then it turns into avoidance. A cycle can be established that can trigger or create more related trauma.

Allyson: Over the years I have witnessed individuals who are not trauma informed. They tell individuals or communities to just deal with it, put on their boots and keep walking. This is always so disheartening. While I do not agree with this sentiment, I do recognize that we cannot stay in the bottomless pit. We must emerge from trauma at some point. And the focus must be on healing from trauma and the future. Maria Yellow Horse Brave Heart writes about this in her work on collective trauma and losses among Indigenous peoples.

Dee: Yes, that is true. She recommends transcending the collective trauma and looking ahead toward the future. There is a legacy of significant trauma and grief in our tribal communities. We must deal with the trauma responses and reactions before we can rightfully reclaim our roles as sacred people, as star people. The lingering effects of trauma are not always visible to the naked eye. People do not know what path you have been on, what you have experienced, and how this impacts your ability to practice resilience, have hope, and walk on a healing path. We are sacred people, coming from the stars but our history contradicts this belief; we are on a pathway of shame not a pathway of sacredness.

Allyson: T.D. Jakes is one of my favorite preachers of all time. I first listened to him at the Global Leadership Summit in 2018. A message that I took with me from this presentation was we must dream big, and not look back at where we started, we always have to look toward the future. Traumatic events can keep us stuck in places we do not want to be. Traumatic events hit our souls and spirits. So many of our stories keep us stuck … I was sexually abused, my parents mistreated me, I grew up homeless, I was beat by my grandfather, I was not loved, I was an orphan. There are more stories. These stories are often shared in therapy, 12-step meetings, and talking circles. I get tired of the stories because they do not tell me anything about the future, where we want to be. We really have to speak our future into existence. We have to let go of trauma.

Dee: When considering trauma, it is essential to consider the population we are working with, or that we want to reach. The first step in addressing trauma is ensuring that it does not happen in the first place, so it is all about prevention. However, we know that trauma is embedded in humankind, we move through the trauma continuum, we must consider interactions, those at risk, those who opt for treatment, and those who are placed in residential treatment or institutions (such as prisons). Relapse, walking outside of the healing path is common during the recovery period, and eventually we hope that individuals can re-enter and regain their place on the healing path. This approach requires connection, support, and intentionality within community-based programs, families, and social-service organizations.

Treating Trauma in Clinical Settings

Stages of trauma recovery in a clinical settings often follow three distinct stages. In stage 1, the focus is on securing safety, stabilizing symptoms, and fostering self-care. In stage 2, reconstructing the trauma and transforming the traumatic memories is the focus. In the final stage, treatment supports the reconciliation with self, others, and resolving the trauma (Herman, 2002).

Stage 1: Establish safety
Stage 2: Remembrance and mourning
Stage 3: Reconnection

There are multiple approaches used to treat trauma and move through these stages. Many clinical treatments are based on evidence and measurable outcomes. For example, **Trauma-Focused Cognitive Behavior Therapy (TF-CBT)** is an evidence-based treatment for trauma. It is based on cognitive behavior (e.g., thinking, feeling, doing), humanistic principles, attachment, neurobiology, and integrating family systems to decrease trauma symptoms. **Parent-child Interaction Therapy** (PCIT) is based on attachment, social learning, parenting style, and externalizing behavior problems (e.g., defiance or aggression). PCIT increases social skills and cooperation while improving parent-child attachment relationships. **Relaxation Techniques** can help lower the body's alarm reaction to trauma. It also reduces distress related to trauma triggers. Common relaxation techniques taught in clinical settings include diaphragmatic breathing, progressive muscle relaxation, visualization, grounding, and naturally relaxing activities, and mindful breathing practices. **Mindfulness and meditation based strategies.** These focus on the mind and the present moment. While multiple forms of mindfulness exist, with trauma-informed mindfulness, the goal is to improve self-regulation and reduce symptoms associated with trauma. One example is grounding and anchoring. In this process, individuals use their five senses to connect and remain in the present moment. **Eye movement desensitization and reprocessing (EMDR)** is used to treat trauma and focuses on past memories, present issues, and future actions. EMDR identifies and addresses experiences that impact the brain's natural resilience (*What Is EMDR?*, 2019). **Energy therapies** work to reduce emotional feelings and unwanted responses to certain memories. Based on the idea that our bodies are made up of energy, the flow of energy may help us overcome trauma and lead to wellbeing. Sometimes the terms Chi, Shakti, or spirit are used in energy work. One example of an energy therapy is emotional freedom techniques (EFT). This includes tapping on a meridian point to target and resolve problems related to trauma. To treat anxiety, a clinician may tap under the eye, arm, and end of the collarbone. In addition to tapping, the individual receiving the treatment practices nine things: close eyes, open eyes, move eyes down and to one side, move eyes down to other side, circle eyes in one direction, then the other, hum a familiar tune, count to five and hum again. EFT is thought to work because it stimulates certain parts of the brain (Marzillier, 2014). **Narrative therapies** include writing about traumatic events and emotions associated with them can help reduce PTSD symptom severity. In clinical settings, individuals may create a representation of their life using a rope, beginning when they were born, and ending in the present. The remaining part of the rope that is not unravelled is the future. Individuals place positive emotive items on the rope for events that are happy, and negative emotive items for sad or fear inducing events. Similar to the imagery methods, this approach seeks to reduce stress and anxiety related to trauma. When completed an individual may write a narrative of their lives using the events presented on the rope, during sessions. **Imagery methods** focus on individual work with a therapist to walk through a traumatic experience with their eyes closed, describing the sequence of events in the order that they occurred. They talk about the trauma, what they see, hear, and feel. The theory behind imagery methods is that as individuals repeatedly relive an event, they will become less anxious about it (Marzillier, 2014). **Pharmacotherapy** is also used to treat and resolve trauma but requires treatment and a prescription from a medical provider.

Allyson: We use the term cognitive coping a lot when talking about trauma and treatment. Can you give me some examples of what cognitive cooping looks like?

Dee: In our traditional teachings there are many examples of cognitive coping. Consider the instruction given when entering a lodge or a ceremony, to leave bad thoughts at the door and enter in a good way. We use imagery to send away unhelpful thoughts. We visualize stories of places and animals, smudging, or family members. It is essential to practice cognitive coping regularly to stay on a healing path.

Trauma and the Spirit

Trauma walks with us on the healing path. There are many ways to heal, to grow and transform through traumatic events. Religious coping, spirituality, and faith-based approaches decrease psychological stress (Bryant-Davis & Wong, 2013). Spiritual practices also increase our ability to forgive and find meaning and satisfaction in life after trauma (Redmond, 2014).

Dee: Our soul/spirit is impacted, we lose faith, our sense of self-worth, we feel helpless and hopeless. Evidence of trauma on the healing path appears in our mind and body. In our soul, trauma might present as loss of purpose and pleasure, feeling helpless and hopeless, or loss of faith, a crisis of the spirit.

Researchers have explored the spiritual practices and mental well-being of combat veterans. Veterans have one of the poorest treatment completion rates and are at high risk for suicide and substance abuse. Many veterans experience PTSD related to their time in combat. A review of 43 studies demonstrates that spirituality decreases PTSD, suicide, depression, anger, anxiety, and improves quality of life in veteran populations (Smith-MacDonald et al., 2017) (Figure 3.2).

Theories on Trauma

Theories on trauma attempt to explain, treat, resolve, and heal. Before a traumatic event occurs, we may be walking on a healing path, this path becomes disrupted with trauma and creates stress. Trauma prevents our basic needs from being met.

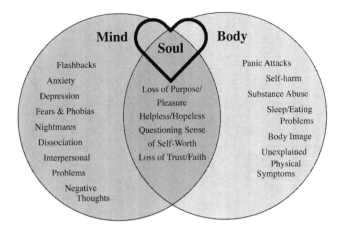

Figure 3.2 Mind, Body and Soul.

Karina Walters and Jane Simoni developed the Indigenist Stress Coping Model and over the years we have used this model a lot to explore how trauma influences health, and how culture moderates trauma. Trauma creates stress. And, we know that trauma can result from historical trauma, discrimination, traumatic life events, and physical and sexual assaults and abuse (Walters & Simoni, 2002). Cultural buffers can lessen undesirable impacts from trauma. Cultural buffers may be identity, enculturation, spiritual coping, or traditional practices. This model can be used with non-indigenous populations and contexts using the same theoretical lens, but different moderators. For example, spirituality or faith-based moderators, community and conditions, and others, Figure 3.3.

The **socioecological model** is another way of understanding how trauma may be addressed through evidence-based treatments. We use this model in our work with communities and it's essential for understanding how to prevent ACEs at all levels, from individual, family, community, and structures, Figure 3.4.

Ecological models stress the interpersonal, intrapersonal, structural factors that contribute to the subjective experiences of healing and recovery (both positive and negative). Within an ecological model of psychological trauma, trauma occurs, this includes a person, event, and ecology/environment (Harvey, 1996). An individual or community has a trauma response to the event. They may seek therapy or professional treatment, or they may not. Some individuals recover psychologically, without treatment. There are several explanations about why some people recover. Within the ecological model, psychological trauma is viewed as a multi-dimensional experience and recovery looks like this.

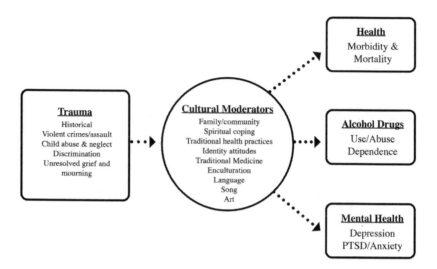

Figure 3.3 Spiritual Moderators and Wellness.

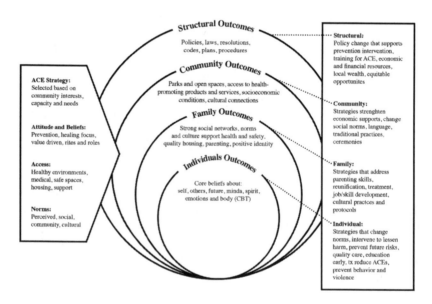

Figure 3.4 Socio Ecological Model and Trauma Response.

- Choosing to recall or note recall traumatic events and identify feelings and memories about the past and the present.
- Feelings associated with the traumatic event are named and discussed without being overwhelming or distressing.
- Triggers or flashbacks are mastered by healthy coping routines, reducing exposure to stressful events, and practicing mindfulness.
- Self-esteem and self-cohesion are restored, feelings of guilt, shame, loss are replaced with self-worth.
- Relationships are possible with the ability to trust, love, and be vulnerable.
- Trauma has new meaning. Rather than asking, "Why did this happen to me?" survivors find meaning and affirmation from the traumatic experience.

One of the scriptures that comes to mind is Luke 19:10, For the Son of Man came to seek out and to save the lost. And, to recover and fully walk on a healing path we must address personal and social conditions that created trauma, addiction, and despair in our lives.

Cognitive and psychodynamic theories are often used in the trauma milieu. Both focus on the mind and individual differences in trauma reactions that occur (Marzillier, 2014).

We are working on the validation of a Tribal Adverse Childhood Experiences tool (TACE) for a client now. This tool balances ACEs with resilience and protective factors in three American Indian communities. In our work leading up to the development of the TACE, we explored how theories, evidence and tribal practices could be used to prevent or moderate ACEs, Figure 3.5.

Research

Adverse Childhood Experiences (ACEs)

What was intuitively assumed by the general public that kids that had a hard time growing up in instable families would end up dead, in prison, or having a hard life has proven to be true with science (research).

Adverse experiences during childhood impact adult health risk behaviors and disease. One of the biggest research studies and contributions to our understanding of trauma came from the ACEs study at Kaiser Permanente's San Diego Health Appraisal Clinic with 45,000 adults. Adult patients completed the ACE Study questionnaire that included questions about their childhood, abuse, and exposure to household dysfunction (trauma). ACE categories included psychological (e.g., Did a parent often or very often swear at, insult, or put you down?), physical (e.g., Did a parent or other adult in the household often or very often push, grab, shove, or slap you?), sexual (Did an adult or person at least 5 years older ever touch or fondle you in a sexual way?), substance abuse (e.g., live with anyone who was a problem drinker or alcoholic?), mental illness

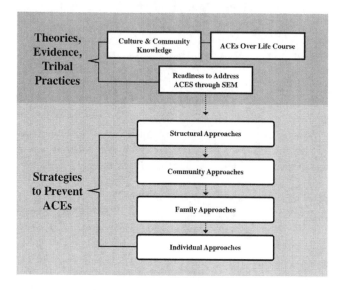

Figure 3.5 Strategies to Prevent ACEs.

(e.g., Was a household member depressed or mentally ill?), mother treated violently (e.g., Was your mother or stepmother ever repeatedly hit over at least a few times?), criminal behavior (e.g., Did a household member go to prison?). Substance abuse exposure was the most common ACE reported by 26% of respondents in the initial ACE study. Sexual abuse was the second most common with 22% of respondents reporting yes to at least one statement regarding sexual abuse (Felitti et al., 1998). Felitti and colleagues found that as the number of ACEs increased, the prevalence and risk for smoking, severe obesity, physical inactivity, depressed mood, and suicide attempts also increased. Other disease conditions also increased with ACE exposure, for example individuals with four or more categories of ACEs were 3.9 times more likely to report emphysema, and 2.2 times more likely to report ischemic heart disease, and 1.6 times more likely to report diabetes (Felitti et al., 1998).

The Centers for Disease Control and other prevention agencies are calling for immediate efforts to reduce ACEs. Their work indicates that preventing ACEs could go a long way in helping people heal. According to the CDC's estimates, reducing ACEs in the US population could potentially result in a:

- 44% decrease in depressive disorders
- 24% decrease in heavy drinking
- 15% decrease in unemployment (Centers for Disease Control and Prevention, 2019).

Check out the resources section at the end of this chapter for more information on ACEs and the Kaiser ACE study published by the Centers for Disease Control.

Posttraumatic Growth

It's been 24 years since the initial ACE study. We know without a doubt, that exposure to trauma during childhood has devastating impacts on one's ability to walk on a healing path, toward wholeness. But it is not all bad. **Posttraumatic growth (PTG)** is emerging as an area of research that explains how trauma actually builds emotional resilience. PTG is defined as positive change that comes from a traumatic event. PTG is rooted in the concept of salutogenesis, or how people stay healthy when they experience stress. This is in sharp contrast to pathogenesis, or the focus on causes of disease (Antonovsky, 1979). Researchers identified five areas of PTG that are essential for understanding how people move from trauma to healing.

- Knowing that new opportunities will come that were not present before the traumatic event happened
- Closer relationships and connections with other people, especially those who suffer
- Increase sense of strength in one's own abilities to face challenges
- Greater appreciation for life and living
- Changes in one's belief system and spiritual practices (Posttraumatic Growth Research Group, 2013).

Dee: Yes, we must consider not only trauma, but also the growth that comes from trauma. This looks different depending on who you are and what you have experienced.

Allyson: I agree. I was talking with a student from Appalachia about trauma, and growth that comes from traumatic experiences. With family members who were prisoners of war, concentration camp survivors, and limited access to healing resources, many family members never healed. I asked her why. She talked about pride, not wanting to admit trauma, not wanting to face it. Education was part of this, limited knowledge about the resources available, that healing and growth can happen. I had to agree. Many people walk to their grave without addressing the traumatic events that have happened to them, they never get to a place of growth and healing.

One of the most traumatic events in recent US history was the World Trade Center bombings. Researchers explored PTG among 4934 survivors of the 9/

11 terrorist attack and indicators of psychological wellbeing (Pollari et al., 2021). They found that PTG was present among survivors 15 years after the attacks. Being female, a racial minority, and having less education were associated with having medium to high PTG. These findings are consistent with other research, where PTG is more prominent among individuals and groups who experience greater lifetime exposures to trauma, and therefore more opportunities to grow and heal.

Dee: Yes, there is an entire generation that has never experienced 9/11 it has been 26 years. I chose not to listen to the tributes and memories about 9/11. It would be really sad. Some people needed to. Being able to have choice is important. It is not that I am ignoring 9/11, there are always reminders of 9/11. These reminders do not set you back to square one. It is the ability to reground yourself when something like this happens. Every time there is a school shooting, parents who have lost a child, they go back, but this set back is not the same as the initial one. How to people get to that point? Regrounding and repurpose are the ingredients that people need to have hope for the future.

Another area of trauma and PTG that demands attention is sexual victimization. Researchers explored sexual violence victimization and PTG among female victims based on 6,187 published articles from 2010 to 2020. Self-reflection and participating in meaningful activities supported positive change and growth. Another area that encouraged PTG among this group was altruistic actions and activism to prevent sexual violence (Guggisberg et al., 2021).

Allyson: This is really interesting. When I started working at the National Center on the Sexual Behavior of Youth (NCSBY) I did this because it was an opportunity to write, conduct qualitative research, and make a difference. But I really believe that it was through this opportunity that I came to talk about my own experiences as a victim of sexual abuse. I recall meeting with some friends, talking with you, talking about being sexually abused during my childhood. I came to realize that this was part of the healing path, but it was also one of the reasons why I could not trust the world and those around me.

Dee: Yes. There is a sacred path that we are on. This path presents opportunities that help us with our own healing. It was not just altruistic, your work with NCSBY was also about your own healing, a form of PTG.

Researchers explored the impact of school shootings on disruptive behaviors in 12 schools located in Oregon. They enrolled students over a three-year period from 1991 to 2006. Participants were exposed to a school shooting in 1998 where student students were killed and 25 were wounded. Although students were significantly impacted, disruptive behaviors actually decreased more quickly than researchers expected. This is likely due to PTG and the increase in social support and mental health services made available to students and families during this time (Liao et al., 2015).

For more on PTG check out the resources section at the end of this chapter.

Discrimination, Trauma, Oppression, Social Injustice and Treatment

Trauma prevalence is higher among racial and ethnic minorities. Racial minorities in the US experience more trauma than non-minority groups. Current systems perpetuate traumas through microaggressions, racism, discrimination, and bias where minority groups do not have the same opportunities for healing. Police shootings and hate crimes against Asian-Americans are traumatic. Many racial minorities experience vicarious trauma when watching or hearing about police brutality, unfair treatment in the prison systems, and various hate crimes.

Allyson: Last year I was teaching a class, Public Health and Social Justice. Students were undergraduate health majors and the majority were African American. This was just after the murder of George Floyd and the police brutality trials. Many had not seen the actual video, it was too upsetting to watch. As the class drew to an end, students said they wanted to watch it. Of course, this was not required, but many stayed to watch the actual video. I could feel the apprehension and tension before the video started. During the video, it was silent, with no words just emotional reactions with heads shaking in disbelief. After the video, it was silent for a bit, then students started talking. Tears were shed.

Dee: Well, I think it is important to be aware of what is happening in our country. Police brutality, racial profiling, and social injustice are key issues that we must address as a collective group, of healers or individuals that help people on a healing path.

Discrimination

Racial minorities experience discrimination when seeking treatment for unresolved trauma. White privilege is at the core of this with white males historically leading health care and treatment organizations. Many providers lack cultural humility, understanding of implicit bias, and their role in leaving trauma unaddressed in individuals and communities.

The American Psychological Association Division of Trauma Psychology reports that:

- 76% of African Americans report trauma in their lifetime
- 9% of African Americans report PTSD
- 46% of American Indians/Alaska Natives report Intimate Partner Violence
- 34% of American Indians/Alaska Native women report being raped
- 61% of American Indians/Alaska Natives report trauma due to physical assault
- 11% of American Indians/Alaska Natives complete suicide
- 15% of African American children experience child maltreatment
- 28% of American Indian/Alaska Natives experience violent victimization
- 63% of African Americans experience racial and ethnic hate crimes (Llamas et al., n.d.)

Racial and ethnic minorities are less likely to seek or receive treatment for trauma.

After Trauma

One study explored what happened to pastors after they witnessed a traumatic event. Interviews with six pastors documented the rituals they engaged in after the traumatic event, and how the event impacted their perceptions, identity, and spiritual engagement. Pastors used rituals to move through their pain and called attention to the need for compassion and grace, to be seen, to be identified with their pain, and to the steadfast presence of others. By participating in rituals, pastors experienced a renewed sense of hope and trust (2020). When parents experience the traumatic loss of a child, spiritual practices can help move through traumatic grief.

Trauma responses are based on how much of a threat you feel and your relationships. Trauma responses are also based on your perspective.

Trauma informed care (TIC) is an approach that providers often use to ensure their response to clients and patients do not harm and reduce potentially traumatic events from happening in the future. Providers (in emergency room departments, social service organizations, mental health departments, and school-based settings) have an obligation to be trauma informed (Bruce et al., 2018). The Substance Abuse and Mental Health Services Administration calls attention to four primary elements of a TIC approach: 1) realizing the widespread impact of trauma exposure, 2) identifying how trauma may impact patients, families, and staff in this system, 3) responding by applying this knowledge into practice and institutional policies, and 4) preventing re-traumatization. Therefore, the obligation that providers have, is to prevent re-traumatization, and to the extent possible, encourage PTG and wellbeing.

Trauma to Recovery

Trauma is inevitable. Our response to trauma is what makes a difference on the healing path. Do we get mad? Do we grow from our burden? Do we have frustrations? Do we blame ourselves? Do we hate ourselves? Do we accept what has happened and move on? Are we just human? Are we alone, without the help of the Creator or God that we can call on in times of our deepest need? Recovery and PTG is all about getting back on the healing path and finding out what is needed to remain in a healing space and help others along the way. There are many teachings presented here that can help.

Resources

Mental Health Treatment Facility Locator: Toll-Free: 1 (800) 789–2647 (English & Española); TDD: 1 (866) 889–2647 http://findtreatment.samhsa.gov/MHTreatmentLocator

Trauma Websites

Asian Americans: http://www.mysahana.org/resources/

Native Americans: Native American survivor and caregiver resources: http://www.giftfromwithin.org/html/amindian.html

Latinos: Website focused on trauma within the Latina/o community: http://transformation-center.org/home/community/community-sub-page2/latino/trauma-brochure-english-01-08-15/

African Americans: Therapist resource directory under the Association of Black Psychologists: http://www.abpsi.org/find-psychologists/

ACEs Connection https://www.acesconnection.com/

Administration for Children and Families https://www.acf.hhs.gov/trauma-toolkit/american-indian-alaskan-native-communities

Centers for Disease Control Kaiser ACE Study https://www.cdc.gov/violenceprevention/aces/about.html

Child Welfare Information Gateway https://www.childwelfare.gov/

National Indigenous Women's Resource Center https://www.niwrc.org/resources

The National Center for Trauma Informed Mental Health www.samhsa.gov/nctic

The National Trauma Consortium (NTC) www.nationaltraumaconsortium.org

The National Child Traumatic Stress Network https://www.nctsn.org/

The Trauma Center at Justice Resource Institute www.traumacenter.org

The National Center on the Sexual Behavior of Youth https://www.ncsby.org/

The University of North Carolina at Charlotte Post Traumatic Growth Research Group https://ptgi.charlotte.edu/what-is-ptg/

Trauma Sensitive Schools https://traumasensitiveschools.org/why/

Books

Shattered Soul? Five Pathways to Healing the Spirit After Abuse and Trauma by Patrick Fleming, Wordstream Publishing, 2011 Nashville, TN. https://www.amazon.com/Shattered-Soul-Pathways-Healing-Spirit/dp/193575808X?asin=193575808X&revisionId=&format=4&depth=1

References

After Trauma Empowerment Network. (2022). *Trauma*. https://www.atenns.ca/trauma.html#/

Antonovsky, A. (1979). *Health, Stress and Coping* (1st edition). Jossey-Bass Inc Pub.

BigFoot, D., & Schmidt, S. (2022). *Honoring Children, Mending the Circle*. Indian Country Child Trauma Center.

Bruce, M. M., Kassam-Adams, N., Rogers, M., Anderson, K. M., Sluys, K. P., & Richmond, T. S. (2018). Trauma Providers' Knowledge, Views and Practice of Trauma-Informed Care. *Journal of Trauma Nursing: The Official Journal of the Society of Trauma Nurses, 25*(2), 131–138. 10.1097/JTN.0000000000000356

Bryant-Davis, T., & Wong, E. C. (2013). Faith to move mountains: Religious coping, spirituality, and interpersonal trauma recovery. *The American Psychologist, 68*(8), 675–684. 10.1037/a0034380

Centers for Disease Control and Prevention. (2019). *Preventing Adverse Childhood Experiences*. National Estimates Based on 2017 BRFSS; Vital Signs, MMWR November 2019. https://www.cdc.gov/vitalsigns/aces/index.html

DeAngelis, T. (2013). Traumatic stress in a violent world. American Psychological Association, *44*(8), 38. https://www.apa.org/monitor/2013/09/traumatic-stress

Felitti, V. J., Anda, R. F., Nordenberg, D., Williamson, D. F., Spitz, A. M., Edwards, V., Koss, M. P., & Marks, J. S. (1998). Relationship of childhood abuse and household dysfunction to many of the leading causes of death in adults. The Adverse Childhood Experiences (ACE) Study. *American Journal of Preventive Medicine, 14*(4), 245–258. 10.1016/s0749-3797(98)00017-8

Guggisberg, M., Bottino, S., & Doran, C. M. (2021). Women's Contexts and Circumstances of Posttraumatic Growth After Sexual Victimization: A Systematic Review. *Frontiers in Psychology, 12.* https://www.frontiersin.org/articles/10.3389/fpsyg.2021.699288

Harvey, M. R. (1996). An ecological view of psychological trauma and trauma recovery. *Journal of Traumatic Stress, 9*(1), 3–23.

Herman, J. L. (2002). Recovery from psychological trauma. *Psychiatry and Clinical Neurosciences, 52*(S1), S98–S103. 10.1046/j.1440-1819.1998.0520s5S145.x

Hirschberger, G. (2018). Collective Trauma and the Social Construction of Meaning. *Frontiers in Psychology, 9*, 1441. 10.3389/fpsyg.2018.01441

Liao, Y., Shonkoff, E. T., Barnett, E., Wen, C. K. F., Miller, K. A., & Eddy, J. M. (2015). Brief report: Examining children's disruptive behavior in the wake of trauma – A two-piece growth curve model before and after a school shooting. *Journal of Adolescence, 44*(1), 219–223. 10.1016/j.adolescence.2015.07.011

Llamas, J., Gobin, R., Gustafson, S., Hendricks, K., Marinski, D., & et al. (n.d.). *Trauma and Posttraumatic Stress Disorder in Ethnic Minorities* (pp. 1–9). American Psychological Association. www.apatraumadivision.org/files/57.pdf

Marzillier, J. (2014). *The Trauma Therapies*. Oxford University Press, Incorporated. http://ebookcentral.proquest.com/lib/uncg/detail.action?docID=1742643

National Child Traumatic Stress Network. (2022). *What is a truamatic event?* https://www.nctsn.org/what-is-child-trauma/about-child-trauma

Pollari, C. D., Brite, J., Brackbill, R. M., Gargano, L. M., Adams, S. W., Russo-Netzer, P., Davidov, J., Banyard, V., & Cone, J. E. (2021). World Trade Center Exposure and

Posttraumatic Growth: Assessing Positive Psychological Change 15 Years after 9/11. *International Journal of Environmental Research and Public Health, 18*(1), Article 1. 10.3390/ijerph18010104

Posttraumatic Growth Research Group. (2013). What is PTG? *Posttraumatic Growth Research Group.* https://ptgi.charlotte.edu/what-is-ptg/

Pumariega, A. J., Jo, Y., Beck, B., & Rahmani, M. (2022). Trauma and US Minority Children and Youth. *Current Psychiatry Reports, 24*(4), 285–295. 10.1007/s11920-022-01336-1

Redmond, L. W. (2014). Spiritual coping tools of religious victims of childhood sexual abuse. *The Journal of Pastoral Care & Counseling: JPCC, 68*(1–2), 3.

Richards, T. N., Schwartz, J. A., & Wright, E. (2021). Examining adverse childhood experiences among Native American persons in a nationally representative sample: Differences among racial/ethnic groups and race/ethnicity-sex dyads. *Child Abuse & Neglect, 111*, 104812. 10.1016/j.chiabu.2020.104812

Smith-MacDonald, L., Norris, J. M., Raffin-Bouchal, S., & Sinclair, S. (2017). Spirituality and Mental Well-Being in Combat Veterans: A Systematic Review. *Military Medicine, 182*(11), e1920–e1940. 10.7205/MILMED-D-17-00099

Walters, K. L., & Simoni, J. M. (2002). Reconceptualizing native women's health: An "indigenist" stress-coping model. *American Journal of Public Health, 92*(4), 520–524. 10.2105/ajph.92.4.520

What is EMDR? | Trauma Recovery. (2019, December 11). https://www.emdrhap.org/content/about/what-is-emdr/

Chapter 4

Recovery

Recovery

Reclaiming what has been lost or establishing a secure foundation. This section is all about recovery, transition, hope, forgiveness, expectations, and anticipation.

What is treatment?
What is prevention?
What is recovery or transformation?
Why consider transitions?

Recovery is about finding a way to move through pain. Recovery happens when we are able to recognize that we are powerless over the pain and seek a higher power.

Recovery is a process rather than a one-time event, rather than thinking that "I am healed". Consider the healing path as a forward motion with less focus on the stress and strain and more focus on the near and far horizon with the choice of being assured in the moment. Recovery is about walking on that healing path, but sometimes we stop, we ponder, we pray, we go off path, we get distracted, or we are not living in a way that represents our best self, the person that we want to be, beyond our brokenness. Recovery represents both powerlessness and strength, the contradiction that we often talk about. In order to recover or restore the sense of core self, we have to be broken from something, some experience, addiction, relationship, or history. Recovery actually begins with an awareness that something needs to change. Step 1 of the Twelve Steps is, "We admitted we were powerless over alcohol, that our lives had become unmanageable." While this focuses narrowly on alcohol, this step of awareness and admission applies to other situations as well.

Recovery is a term used in the substance abuse field to articulate the process of positive growth and stability. Recovery definitely means different things to different people. For individuals and consumers of various treatment and recovery programs, recovery is about self-reliance, being able to reduce treatment needs, and returning to our original levels of functioning or living (Corrigan et al., 2019),

DOI: 10.4324/9781003274018-4

or establishing the stability and consistency to feel confidence in living. Researchers define recovery as a personal process of changing one's attitudes, values, feelings, goals, skills, and roles. Recovery is about living a hopeful and meaningful life, even when illness and disease cause setbacks, or the need to recover. For some, the concepts, methods, and understandings that they have about recovery do not come from lived experience, but from textbooks, conferences, training, and professors. And a critical issue about the science of recovery, the evidence base contributing to what we know about how people recover, often comes from researchers without context and the lived experience of recovery.

Over the years we have implemented multiple mental, behavioral, and substance abuse treatment programs and evaluations funded by the Substance Abuse and Mental Health Services Administration. SAMHSA's definition of recovery is based on 10 principles. Recovery is person-driven. It has many pathways. It is holistic, involves peer support, it's relational, cultural, addresses trauma, focuses on strengths and responsibilities, demands respect, and fosters hope. From these 10 principles, there are 4 dimensions necessary for recovery, health, home, purpose, and community. Health is about managing and dealing with a disease or symptoms. In a recovery state of mind, individuals make informed, healthy decisions that support their physical, emotional, and spiritual well-being (SAMHSA, n.d.). Home within the context of recovery is having a stable and safe place to live. Purpose in recovery looks like meaningful activities, independence, income, and resources to contribute and participate in the community. Community in recovery is about relationships and social networks that support, uplift, instill hope, and love.

Guiding Principles of Recovery are outlined below.

- There are many pathways to recovery.
- Recovery is self-directed and empowering.
- Recovery involves a personal recognition of the need for change and transformation.
- Recovery is holistic.
- Recovery has cultural dimensions.
- Recovery exists on a continuum of improved health and wellness.
- Recovery emerges from hope and gratitude.
- Recovery involves a process of healing and redefinition for self and family.
- Recovery is supported by peers and allies.
- Recovery involves (re)joining and (re)building a life in the community.
- Recovery is a reality. It can, will, and does happen (White & Kurtz, 2008)

Allyson: How do we know what we need to recover? Where do we begin? How does a person make their scars beautiful and embrace the experience?

Dee: There are different resources available based on an individual's recovery needs. Therapists, counselors, psychiatrists, and support specialists. But how do we find someone who might be able to help? It is not sitting in the back of someone as they free associate. It is not talking about worldview or least biased foundation. Our assumptions create a reality that is not true or factual. We want to have assumptions that have some validity to understand behaviors. The least biased one is understanding cognition, affect, thinking, and emotions. You cannot measure attitude. You can score a person's perceptions based on what they give you, you can measure behavior.

What are you telling yourself that keeps you from not being well? Can we help you change that story? I want to walk to be healthy. But I do not. I tell myself it is too hot to walk. Is there another form of walking or exercise that would be equivalent? What about walking inside at the YMCA?

Allyson: Recovery is not just sobriety, it is about a transformation of self and relationships. I think the terms that we use to describe recovery mean different things to different people. Many people associate the term recovery with sobriety or being in "long-term recovery". This is a somewhat selfish use of the term recovery because it fails to recognize all of the ways that people recover or need recovery, and not just from substances, but from everything. Writing this book, I was faced head-on with my own brokenness. The idea is that we cannot write and give advice to others about recovery if we have not achieved recovery in some way. Talking with my daughter about a recent recovery post, she said, "Mom you are not in recovery." While I disagree with her, I am in recovery by all textbook and 12-step definitions … She is 12. In her mind recovery is only related to alcohol. She is like many people I have met in my career. "Recovery is not me. I do not need it. There is nothing wrong with me. I am whole." I disagree.

Gabor Mate' says something very similar in his book, "In the Realm of Hungry Ghost," that we can quickly acquire addictive or consuming activities that might appear acceptable, i.e., purchasing books, shoes, cleaning, and travel, but it eventually interferes with relationships, creates a burden, and/or have financial consequences. **Most addictions are the result of trauma.**

Dee: That understanding is essential. You know that something that has been internalized, how we think about recovery and internalize recovery matters since it is the bedrock of turning from choices and justifications of what is not helpful toward a transition of being more in control and knowing better decisions means better outcomes. Is it returning back to something, restoring, or is it growth? Or all of the above?

Allyson: I've been thinking about the concept of reclaiming what's been lost … but then sometimes like, if you're in a horrible relationship, you're recovering from that, and you don't ever want to reclaim that place. Or you decide to reclaim yourself, your purpose, and your place in the sacred circle. It's your spirit and your connection with the Creator through a process of really knowing your place on the healing path. I think we get to a point where we are willing to do anything to recover, anything is better than hitting rock bottom. I think it is that stepping forward. Knowing how and when to step forward. It is where you land after a decision is made to move forward on a healing path, or where you land after a traumatic event occurs. How do we land in a good way, on the other side of trauma?

Dee: Yes. How do you visualize what is opening up to you, on that healing path to start a new journey or recovery journey? Or is that where the leap of faith comes in because you really do not know what will come next? I want to make sure people understand that you still take the experience with you. But it doesn't distort your life. You don't allow the negativity of it to distort your vision, but you still grow from that experience.

The process of recovery is based on unseen faith and hope.

Dee: I remember this one family with six kids, they were members of my church, and of course, for my church there is a huge emphasis on not drinking alcohol. When somebody is an alcoholic in the church, it is seeming more obvious since the contrast is so great. Addiction is a struggle every single solitary day which many find hard to deal with. The kids were really upset with their dad's lying and promises to stay sober which he could not do. The dad was always saying he would stop drinking. This was the struggle over many years. The mom endured all of the drinking and broken promises; the kids did not understand why she put up with him. The oldest son asked, "tell me how you can do this. How can you believe him? You let him keep coming home and he is lying to you." The mom said, "Because at that moment, your dad believed that he could become sober, that he would not drink. That is why I believe him."

We asked our good friend to share a healing story, we wanted to know how he found the healing path. His story *Good Words Are Medicine* tells us that we heal by helping others heal.

Good Words Are Medicine

It's two o'clock in the morning and I've got my feet dangling off the side of a bridge on the rough edge of Toronto's north end. A long way from the prairies and an even longer way from the lakes, and moss and that dense northern bush that invites you in with its long open arms.

There's a bit of twinkle in the dried-up stream below. Struggling its way towards the great lakes I suppose ... But my focus is far from the water now, and on the dark grey rocks a hundred feet downstairs instead.

"Bet I could biff my head off that one right there" I say to Stranger, my shaky finger doing a poor job of pointing it out and holding a smoke at the same time. Behind Stranger are six flashing squad cars behind twelve cops forming a perfect horseshoe; my lucky day I suppose ... Stranger had apparently been holding his flip phone open while I decimated him in a very one-sided debate about the death of evolution, worldwide empathy deficits, and the ubiquity of human suffering. Definitely enough to convince the 9-1-1 dispatcher to send the whole softball team out.

I'd had enough of the distrust and shame, of the night faces and voices, and feeling like I could see the entire lives of each person who walked by. It hadn't been long, but I was tired of the loneliness, the purposelessness, and the heartbreak already too.

Stranger takes his leave as the cops close in and I let him know I'll write about him in a book one day; I'm embarrassed to say I've forgotten his name after that grand gesture and that it's taken more than 20 years to get around to the writing bit. Sorry Stranger.

"Just get down". A very poor choice of words from Cop #2. A victim of budget cuts intended for mental health training I suppose ... I'm thinking up some sassy last words as two hands rush forwards and pull me back onto the concrete. Cuffs, knees, pat down, and wisecracks are next. Not my first rodeo unfortunately. Cop #3 pulls a 26 of rum out of my jacket pocket. "Been drinking have we?" his smirk contorting to a point of perversion. "That's not mine" I reply, and as grade-school obvious a denial as it sounds; it's true. A friend had asked me to carry it into the university bar we ended up at. His rationale was that as an actual student he could be reprimanded or expelled, while I would simply be kicked out of the bar if caught with it. I was honoured to have my lack of life progress be useful for something. I didn't have the will to explain all of this to Cop #3 though, and I had indeed been drinking, just not the rum. I was still young but had already fit a lifetime of wild-wandering years into a just few trips around the Sun, so I decided against any sort of virtue signalling or argumentation on the subject.

I spent the night on the psych ward of some filthy Toronto hospital. The triage nurse, also a victim of those mental health budget cuts I suppose rushing me through the mental status exam like I was interrupting her favourite stories. One too many hours of listening to a woman's sustained screaming from a restraint bed and the intercom says that they're sending in a social worker for a proper assessment. I had been preparing myself on just how to respond to this, deciding what kind of scene to make. Maybe charge the door and see how far I could get, maybe trash the place and chase them out. I'm pretty tired so I settle for being as condescending as possible and coach myself to hate whatever comes through that door. But Guy is wearing flip flops, cargo shorts and a Hawaiian shirt. What the hell? A pack of smokes sticking out of his shirt pocket, shoulder length curly hair and thick black horn-rim glasses long before they became hipster cool again. I was thrown off I suppose … but gather my resolve and remind myself that he is but a cog in the machine. Ignore the funky exterior. I go with a frosty dose of silent treatment as he says hello, introduces himself, and asks how I'm doing. "Is it goblins, fairies or heartbreak then?" Guy says, and I can't resist the urge to look up at him. A soft smile on his face and now on mine. He takes a flamethrower to the snow fort I'd built around my heart and after maybe 10 minutes I'm spilling guts I didn't know I had to spill. What just happening here? I even thanked him as he left. "Thank you?" I said out loud to myself, still dumbfounded by what had occurred. Before I could figure it all out I was released and walking myself home. No longer a risk I suppose …

I'd spend the next few years trying to emulate Guy's magic, breaking up Friday night fights downtown or inviting sad looking folks to join me for dinner. I liked to think about all the ways you could turn someone's attention inward, or outward, or whichever direction it needed to turn in that moment of molten hot anger or bone chilling melancholy. They were everywhere, the masses searching and scratching, tripped up like I was I suppose. Create a common enemy, capitalize on confusion, pop a question about directions, followed by one about their hopes and dreams. Pretending to be an old friend and insisting his name was Bill convinced one fella to drop a brick he was thinking about bludgeoning another man with on Queen Street. Most people are eager to get into the moment with you when they're lost but spend so much time trying to escape it that they forget it's even there.

With each helping experience I felt stronger, I felt like I had done something important, I felt a purpose forming, I felt like I was healing. One part altruism, one part parasite I suppose … So, I pointed my shoes toward behaviour therapy and psychotherapy and ceremony and severe mental illness and incarceration and marginalisation and advocacy and activism.

And so, sitting in this cold lodge on the third night of fasting, I remember leaning forward towards those grey rocks below. I remember the quick hands of that officer on my back. Stranger's flip phone and concerned-compassionate expression, Guy's efflorescent warmth and soft smile, and the good words of many others who would share their medicine at the exact right moment. I feel wave after wave of gratitude crashing over me. We heal by helping others heal, I hear from the fire.

Good words are medicine I suppose.

Research on How People Recover

There has been a shift in what we know about recovery, and how people recover. This shift has dramatically happened in the last two decades and influenced by researchers and policy change, recovery funding, services, research, and advocacy. Researchers explored models of recovery and mental health through a systematic examination of 25 research articles (Dell et al., 2021). They found five themes that help us understand what comprehensive recovery and wellness look like on the healing path. First, they defined recovery. Recovery is a transformation from a negative identity state to a positive state of psychological well-being. This transformation is based on four additional themes: 1) social and environmental conditions support access to basic resources and safety, 2) individuals develop a sense of autonomy and personal responsibility, 3) roles and relationships facilitate personal experiences of belonging and meaning, and 4) individual enlightenment, where individuals accept illness as part of oneself and know how to live in a way that supports wellbeing. Recovery is a transformation from a negative identity state to a positive identity state. Transformational recovery requires individuals in recovery and recovery advocates to:

• Address marginalization
• Understand
• Share
• Trust

Research on Short-Term Recovery

We supported the implementation and evaluation of a peer recovery support program to identify key factors of successful short-term recovery (Kelley et al., 2021). **Short-term recovery** is defined as being in recovery longer than six months. We developed three research questions to explore short-term recovery. First, we wanted to know how recovery capital resources and indicators of recovery differ between participants who completed a six-month follow-up and those who did not. We also explored how much recovery capital resource measures changed between intake and six-month follow-up. The final question was documenting the recovery capital resources associated with short-term balanced recovery. We defined balanced short-term recovery as a composite score with four indicators of change from intake to six-month follow-up, each associated with a component of the Medicine Wheel (Moore & Coyhis, 2010). We utilized the GPRA tool (an instrument required by federal funding agencies) to assess (1) health status (spiritual health), (2) impact of substances on activity (physical health), (3) psychological/emotional impact of substances (emotional health), and (4) days of substance use (mental health). Our findings suggested that when people have a mix of external and internal recovery capital they may be more likely to achieve a more balanced short-term recovery. People who became occupied with school, work, or training or maintained their occupation had more than six times the odds of achieving short-term recovery when compared to those who were not occupied. This may be related to the concept that when individuals feel their life has meaning they are more likely to understand and be able to cope with difficulties while maintaining short-term recovery. Interactions with family and friends were also associated with short-term recovery. Participants who maintained or increased their interactions with family or friends who were supportive of recovery had more than four times the odds of experiencing recovery scores as compared to those with decreased or no interactions. When participants were still receiving services at follow-up they had more than twice the odds of achieving short-term recovery. Not all recovery capital resources were significantly associated with short-term recovery scores. Income change and attendance in recovery groups were not significantly related to balanced recovery in this study.

We know that families, communities, programs, and policies influence how people recover.

Within families, recovery may look like relationships being restored, healthy boundaries, resolved trauma, and addressing co-dependency. The path to recovery does not occur outside of the family, but within. Recovery and healing is a family problem and requires family-based solutions. We cannot expect to find a healing path in places where there is trauma, addiction, abuse, and brokenness; however, that is the world we live in. How do recovery, restoration, and healing occur in the midst of living? How does one walk the path of healing when there is chaos surrounding each step? We will review more on families and recovery in chapter 6.

Restorative justice models are one way, but they are in sharp contrast to retributive justice approaches based on the punishment of offenders, rather than rehabilitation. One village in Alaska brings offenders back into the community, into the sacred circle of life rather than banishing them. The offenders must reconcile and work toward acceptance and forgiveness, but the concept here is that the community is one unit, they support the recovery of both the victim and the offender. Some believe that restorative justice marks an evolution of awareness and knowing within mankind (Rohr, 2021). Policy change and awareness is one way that can happen.

We know that policies support recovery and in the last decade these policies have drastically improved access to and funding for recovery-related services. However, change is still necessary for the policy realm. As a public health and social justice advocate, I demand and advocate for policy change. Current policies fail to support recovery. Here are just a few examples.

- The **Americans with Disabilities Act** (ADA) does not allow employers to treat employees or potential employees differently because of their disabilities. ADA does not recognize current illegal drug use as a disability. Employers may fire, demote, or terminate employees who seek treatment for addiction (Americans with Disabilities Act, ND).
- **Fair Housing Laws** (HUD, ND) negatively impact individuals and families with substance abuse histories. These Laws allow landlords and federal subsidized housing agencies to deny individuals housing because of illegal drug use.
- **42 CFR Part 2 (HIPPA)** allows healthcare providers to share information about patient substance use disorders with law enforcement, judges, and

others who may subpoena the information. There is no requirement for confidentiality during legal proceedings. Sharing information about a patient's disorder may perpetuate stigma, discrimination, and treatment bias in the healthcare system.

But the policy narrative is not all bad, there is hope.

- The **Mental Health Parity and Addiction Equity Act of 2008** (MHPAEA) and the **Affordable Care Act of 2010** (ACA) allow primary care providers to treat substance use disorders like any other disease. Researchers report increases in access to services and reductions in emergency department visits and hospital stays because of these two acts (Volkow et al., 2017).
- The **21st Century Cures ACT of 2016** aims to improve health outcomes for individuals with mental illness and substance use disorders who have been released from prison (Cole et al., 2018) and advocates for decriminalizing substance abuse through a public health approach and addressing racial disparities that plague the US criminal justice system.
- The **Substance Use-Disorder Prevention that Promotes Opioid Recovery and Treatment for Patients and Communities Act of 2018 (SUPPORT)** aims to address the US opioid crisis. Key provisions in the Act include grants, first responder training, comprehensive opioid recovery centers, best practices for recovery housing, and common indicators to identify fraudulent recovery housing operators (SAMHSA, n.d.).

Allyson: These policies and laws make me think about some of the participants or clients who show up in treatment programs. Many are required to be there, court ordered. I think this is one of the reasons we have a revolving door when it comes to the criminal justice systems, relapse, reincarceration, and recovery. Prisons do not prepare people to leave or walk on a healing path. When people leave prison, some are given gate money. But gate money is never enough to actually find a house, transportation, food, or prepare for a job. If you are living in Alabama, you might receive $10 when you are released at the gate, in California, up to $200. This is not enough to support individuals on the healing path. What happens is that they end up homeless. They try to find a job but no one will hire them because they are felons. Even if they earn enough money for rent, many cannot find places to rent because of the Fair Housing Laws, that are not fair or just. The cycle is so obvious to me, they go back to staying in a hotel or on the streets for a few nights. The only way to make money is often illegal, selling drugs, stealing, prostitution … we wonder why people have a difficult time with recovery.

Dee: Poverty is a contributor to poor recovery. The support systems are not sufficient; there are gaps and limitations in which those that need the help the most are less likely to receive the leave of support for them to truly be helped.

Recovery Services

Some people access recovery, or a healing path through 12-step groups, AA and NA programs, recovery coaching, recovery housing, recovery management, recovery community centers, and recovery-based education. The common thread linking all of these services is that they support individuals in recovery using a variety of methods. Support may be in the form of information, emotional support, general services, or connection between groups and communities (Kelley, 2022).

12-Steps and Alcoholics Anonymous (AA) and Narcotics Anonymous (NA)

One of the most well-known recovery organizations is AA. Founded in 1939, AA is the largest alcohol and drug-related 12-step program in the world (Sussman, 2010). AA is a self-governing, nonprofit organization whose only requirement for membership is a desire to stop drinking (Galanter, 2007). AA programs utilize approaches informed by cognitive behavioral therapy (CBT) and motivational treatment (MT), but not in a clinical setting. Developed following principles of the Oxford Group, a religious organization that wanted to replicate Christianity but without doctrine, the 12-step programs today welcome all people and faiths while promoting the concept of a higher power and spiritual experiences. As one of the most widely known and used recovery support programs, AA is located in 150 countries and includes more than 2 million members (White & Kurtz, 2008).

The 12-steps of AA include the following:

1   We admitted we were powerless over alcohol – that our lives had become unmanageable.
2   Came to believe that a Power greater than ourselves could restore us to sanity.
3   Made a decision to turn our will and our lives over to the care of God as we understood Him.
4   Made a searching and fearless moral inventory of ourselves.
5   Admitted to God, to us, and to another human being the exact nature of our wrongs.
6   Were entirely ready to have God remove all these defects of character.
7   Humbly asked Him to remove our shortcomings.

8 Made a list of all persons we had harmed and became willing to make amends to them all.
9 Made direct amends to such people wherever possible, except when doing so would injure them or others.
10 Continued to take personal inventory and when we were wrong promptly admitted it.
11 Sought through prayer and meditation to improve our conscious contact with God as we understood Him, praying only for knowledge of His will for us and the power to carry that out.
12 Having had a spiritual awakening as the result of these steps, we tried to carry this message to alcoholics and to practice these principles in all our affairs (Alcoholics Anonymous, 2016, p. 1)

Since AA's inception in 1939, several recovery programs have replicated AA such as Narcotics Anonymous (NA), Self-Management and Recovery Training (SMART), Women for Sobriety, Rational Recovery, Secular Organization for Sobriety, and LifeRing Secular Recovery. The goal of 12-step programs may be misunderstood by mainstream society. Fr. Richard Rohr writes about emotional sobriety and the goal of the 12-steps. Emotional sobriety is the goal, the goal is not abstinence from alcohol. The 12-steps help individuals become spiritually awakened person who has been able to detach from their own emotional, and narcissistic responses (Rohr, 2022).

Medicine Wheel/White Bison

White Bison advocates for **the Four Laws of Change** in their recovery model, including 1) change comes from within, 2) for development to occur, it must be preceded by a vision, 3) a great learning must occur, and 4) you must create a healing forest. The Medicine Wheel/White Bison approach is widely used throughout Indian Country. The Medicine Wheel stress the importance of balance and the mental, spiritual, emotional, and physical aspects of well-being as they relate to recovery. The Medicine Wheel and 12-step programs are designed in a series of modules that enable people to meet their individual needs. For example, steps 1 through 3 focus on Finding the Creator; steps 4–6 focus on Finding Yourself; steps 7–9 focus on Finding Your Relationship with others; steps 10–12 focus on Finding the Wisdom of the Elders (Kemppainen et al., 2008). The Medicine Wheel approach strengthens social and emotional bonds among participants and fosters emotional, mental, physical, and spiritual growth (White Bison, n.d.). A key difference between the Medicine Wheel program and a 12-step program is the incorporation of Native values and spirituality. For example, each step includes a value that participants embrace, such as honesty, hope, faith, courage, integrity, humility, and service.

12 Step Steps for Men (White Bison, n.d.)

- Finding the Creator – Steps 1, 2, 3
- Finding Yourself – Steps 4, 5, 6
- Finding Your Relationship With Others – Steps 7, 8, 9
- Finding the Wisdom of Elders – Steps 10, 11, 12

White Bison's Wellbriety and Firestarter Curriculum

White Bison implemented a peer-designed and peer-delivered curriculum from 1998 to 2008 based on Native American traditional values and the Four Laws of Change for Wellbriety mentioned previously. Peer leaders, also called Firestarter's, were trained to mobilize and implement change in their communities (Moore & Coyhis, 2010). Working to empower local communities to provide peer support, recovery support services, prevention, address stigmatization, and increase local resources, the Wellbriety program model reported positive outcomes, crime-free lifestyle increased by 3.2%, employment and or school enrollment increased by 6.4%, and negative substance related personal social consequences improved 3.3% (Moore & Coyhis, 2010).

Healing Forest Concept

White Bison and other social theorists advocate for the concept of a healing forest. The Healing Forest model is based on the idea that if one tree in a forest is sick and removed, and brought back to health, then returned to a sick forest, the tree will become sick again. Healing communities require everyone's participation in the healing process. Moore and Coyhis advocate that this is the only way systemic change will occur. The roots of the forest must address anger, guilt, shame, and fear. The new roots must be based on culture and spirituality (Moore & Coyhis, 2010). The soil and conditions surrounding the forest must be healthy, vibrant, nutrient-dense, feeding the roots so that every tree thrives.

Recovery Homes and Housing

Recovery homes are where healing can begin. Sometimes we refer to Recovery Homes as RH, these support individuals in recovery and are classified using four levels.

- Level 1 RHs are self-run without support from professionals.
- Level 2 RHs have a peer or professional on-site to support recovery-related activities and services.
- Level 3 RHs include professionals in the home, clinical services, and service coordination.

• Level 4 RHs are generally licensed with clinical services, state-funded services, court-mandated living, and often times coordinate services with larger instructions (Jason et al., 2021).

One of the most popular recovery housing program approaches is Oxford House (Oxford House, n.d.). Oxford Houses are recovery homes for individuals with substance abuse histories and there are more than 1,200 of them in the U.S. (Jason et al., 2021). The Oxford House Model is based on the following guidelines:

1 May be democratically self-run
2 Membership is responsible for all expenses
3 Individuals in recovery may live in the house as long as they do not drink alcohol, use drugs, and pay equal expenses
4 If anyone uses substances they are expelled
5 Average stay is about a year, but some people stay up to three years
6 Houses are men-only or women-only houses
7 Applications to live in houses are received by existing members of the house
8 Houses have six to ten members
9 No limits placed on sobriety, some individuals are sober for five days, others 30 or more (Jason et al., 2021)

Studies on the Oxford House model show that substance use, and criminal activity decreased, and employment improved for individuals living in an Oxford House compared with individuals assigned to "usual care" (Jason et al., 2021). An essential part of the Oxford House model is the recovery support network that is available to residents. Recovery support networks provide mentoring, support for abstinence-related goals, and self-improvement, all of which support long-term recovery. Long-term studies of RH's report that when residents are engaged in 12-step groups they are more likely to maintain long-term recovery (Borkman et al., 1998). Research also suggests that when individuals have access to clinical support and stay longer in RHs, they have better outcomes than individuals who do not have clinical support or shorter stays (Polcin et al., 2010).

Dee: Recovery houses and recovery support are important to the healing path; they seem to be what some people need to create and live in conditions that promote recovery and healing.

Allyson: Not always. Over the years I have seen people who have entered recovery homes following discharge from residential treatment. Sometimes living with a group of individuals with addiction is not the solution and it really does not work. One of the cases I remember is a woman leaving residential treatment for alcohol addiction. She was placed in a recovery home near the treatment facility. She lived with five other women, all in recovery, and at different stages. One of the women relapsed while at home. She began using fentanyl again. The four other women in the house relapsed shortly after her, and one never tried fentanyl before. She fatally overdosed. She did not recover and now has no chance to recover. So while I love the concept of recovery homes, I am cautious to say that they actually work for everyone. We must consider that what is helpful for one person may not be helpful for another. There is a balance between recognizing the power of addiction and self-empowerment.

Five Rules of Recovery

Steven Melemis writes about his 30 years of work with patients and common rules they follow to maintain their recovery or walking in the desired direction on the healing path.

Rule #1 change your life
Rule #2 be completely honest
Rule #3 ask for help
Rule #4 practice self-care
Rule #5 don't bend the rules (Melemis, 2015)

Families as Recovery Support Systems

We recognize that families play an essential role in the recovery process and are systems within themselves. When families participate in recovery, individuals are more likely to adhere to treatment regimens and have positive recovery outcomes compared with individuals without family support (Kennedy & Horton, 2011). Researchers in New Mexico interviewed behavioral health agencies to explore family systems that support recovery. They found that families provide the following types of assistance to their relatives in recovery: being there, emotional or moral aid, encouraging social activity, encouraging treatment, feedback, financial, general, going to appointments, childcare, housing, listening, making appointments, reading, writing, match, forms, socializing, self-care, transportation, understanding, and other types of assistance (Kennedy & Horton, 2011).

Social Media

Social media may help or hinder recovery on the healing path. **Social Media and Networks** and social capital are predictors of health and well-being. Social factors are associated with alcohol and drug abuse (both recovery and relapse). Researchers explored social ties and networks in a national sample of adults with varying use and social networking characteristics (Mowbray et al., 2014). Individuals without an alcohol use disorder history had the largest social networks and individuals with alcohol use disorder reported the smallest social networks (Mowbray et al., 2014; Mericle, 2014; Owens & McCrady, 2014). Social environments impact alcohol or drug relapse in persons recently released from jail (Owens & McCrady, 2014). Adult males' social networks change after spending time in jail and social networks predict an individual's future substance use. One month after being released from jail, adult males are more likely to continue their pattern of substance use if they keep the same social networks (Owens & McCrady, 2014). But people in early recovery should be careful about engaging with social media and what they post on various social media platforms (Smith, 2019). When individuals post about their recovery online, they may be subject to stigmatization, judgment, and employer reviews of online presence and activities. Recovery.org encourages people to post on social media in a closed group with members that individuals know (Smith, 2019). At the end of the day, it's up to the individual to determine how active they want to be on social media while considering how this helps or hinders them on the healing path.

We know that during the COVID-19 pandemic, individuals in recovery reported stress, isolation, limited access to health care, difficulty accessing treatment, and lack of structure as key factors that threaten their recovery (McDonnell et al., 2021). Treatment programs switched to online groups, telehealth sessions, and one-on-one chats as opposed to in-person sessions. Social media and virtual sessions were instrumental in connecting people to wellness resources.

Digital Recovery Support Services (D-RSS) tools are increasingly being used to support individuals through telehealth platforms, recovery apps, and remote monitoring (wearable devices). Some examples of D-RSS include websites, digital recovery forums, social networking sites based on recovery, smartphone applications, and text messaging programs. Although researchers do not have convincing evidence that D-RSS promote recovery-related outcomes, they are widely used. A recent study reports that at least 11% of US adults who are in recovery from a substance use disorder have used at least one D-RSS tool (Ashford et al., 2020). One clear benefit of D-RSS is they eliminate barriers that many experience when seeking recovery such as confidentiality, anonymity, scheduling conflicts, childcare, work schedules, transportation, and others. A systematic review of D-RSS users found that low-income individuals were more likely to use D-RSS than a national recovery study sample (Bergman et al., 2018).

Theories on Recovery

One of the most widely used models in recovery is the **transtheoretical model of health behavior change** (Prochaska & DiClemente, 1983;

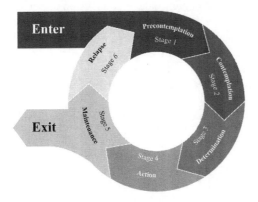

Figure 4.1 Stages of Change and the Healing Path.
Source: Adapted from Prochaska and DiClemente, 1984; SAMHSA, 1999.

Prochaska & Velicer, 1997). We've used this a lot in our work, it's sometimes referred to as the stages of change model. The model is based on six stages of recovery that individuals move through as they are wanting to change behaviors associated with undesirable behavior, this could be drug and alcohol use, consuming an unhealthy diet, or unhealthy relationships. We can visualize this model, and these steps on the healing path, Figure 4.1.

- Stage 1 – precontemplation. In this stage, an individual may not be aware of their behavior and they may not want to change.
- Stage 2 – contemplation. Individuals may think about wanting to change, and they see negative consequences from their behaviors (relationships, illness, criminal justice involvement), but at this stage, an individual is not willing to change. Some individuals contemplate changing their entire lives, but never get to the next stage.
- Stage 3 – preparation. In this stage, an individual starts to create a plan of action based on what they need. This could be inpatient or outpatient treatment, 12-step programs, recovery support, or therapy.
- Stage 4 – action. The action stage is when visible movement begins on the healing path, a decision is made to do something to recover and heal.
- Stage 5 – maintenance. After action, it is essential to maintain new behaviors, decisions, and skills and continue on the healing path. In this stage there may be steps taken in the wrong direction on the healing path, an individual might stop, look back. During the maintenance stage, individuals learn to live and walk on a healing path, they recognize their gifts and talents, they feel confident, called, and connected to a higher purpose and power.

- Stage 6 – termination. This is the stage where some people feel healed, recovered, or complete. The impacts of addiction and trauma are no longer leading an individual down a path they do not want to walk on. For individuals with addiction, cravings often disappear, for individuals with a heightened vigilance or traumatic response to certain events, this will decrease or disappear. Individuals maintain for a lifetime. This is the goal at least.

Most programs do not treat addiction or the problem at a spiritual level. One addiction is often exchanged for another. For example, alcohol for food. Experts believe that addiction will continue to happen, and treatment and recovery approaches will continue to fail unless they treat the issue as a spiritual one (Miskelly, 2018). Citing the work of the United Methodist Church, Miskelly calls for addressing issues of sin, brokenness, attachment, and denial (2018). However, many people are weary, they are not convinced that the solution to recovery is a spiritual one, choosing to think of recovery more as physical. Recovery is so much more than abstinence.

Allyson: I love the representation of the butterfly, the story it represents, we are always becoming. Recovery is ongoing learning, self-revelation. This is where self-help, sponsorship, positive self-talk, checking in, writing, journaling, mediation, and reflection show-up.

Dee: Yes. We must implement, establish, maintain practices that support wellness. When you are on this healing path, it is easy to get discouraged. All of these helpers, that is the tools we have access to, – these can help with that discouragement or when we feel undermined. How do we have strategies to help us be as successful as possible? We do this with finances, weight loss, goal setting, schools, studying, etc. How do we come up with ways of approaching something that has the outcome that what we want? How do we maximize our time? Prioritize relationships? Making sure that opportunities are available. What is the benefit of keeping with the narrative that is in my head? Is it repeating a story that allows me to be empowered or do I feel helpless by that internal dialogue? What benefits are there in repeating the same story over and over again? What kind of shift in the story is necessary that makes for a recovery ending?

Allyson: Yes, it is all in the story. We create stories about ourselves and what other people think about us, and what we think is happening with others. For example, I have a family member deep in addiction. I see their story every day and I know they could benefit from recovery, walking on a healing path, but they do not see it, it is not part of their story … yet.

Dee: Some people are one dimensional, they are just concerned with one thing, when people are living in a one dimensional state, the spiritual realm is not accessible to them. The spiritual realm is necessary for recovery to happen, to find truth, meaning, and purpose.

Research and Interventions for Recovery

Much has been done to research how people recover. Spirituality, mindfulness therapy, music therapy, art therapy, drumming therapy, complementary alternative medicine, and integrative approaches to name a few. While we cannot capture all of the research, these are the areas we feel have the greatest potential to heal and transform.

Spirituality

People in recovery experience a spiritual transformation, a belief in an unseen and higher power. Step 12 of AA is, "Having had a spiritual awakening as the result of these Steps, we tried to carry this message to alcoholics, and to practice these principles in all our affairs." Spirituality in the recovery world may be thought of as social connections, meaning and purpose, relationships, awareness, and beliefs in a higher power. Researchers developed the **spirituality in recovery or SIR framework** to explore spirituality as a process of converting personal values into actionable behaviors. Healthy behaviors lead to a recovery path and help individuals as they deal with personal problems and conflicts that may take them away from their recovery (Brown et al., 2019).

Mindfulness Therapy

Mindfulness is one of the most popular interventions in the recovery milieu. Garland and colleagues explored mindfulness-oriented recovery enhancement for chronic pain and prescription opioid misuse in a randomized control trial (RCT) (2014). They randomized 115 patients with chronic pain into a treatment and control group and assessed outcomes at pre and post-treatment, and three months after the intervention (Garland et al., 2014). They explored changes in opioid use status and desire for opioids, stress, nonreactivity, and reappraisal. Findings from their RCT demonstrate the feasibility and efficacy of mindfulness as an effective approach and treatment for addressing co-occurring prescription opioid misuse, stress, and chronic pain.

Music Therapy

Music therapy is an evidence-based treatment that helps individuals recover and heal from mental, spiritual, physical, and emotional disorders and diseases. In a music therapy session, individuals may create music, sin, listen, dance, talk about music lyrics, or even play an instrument. One study investigated the use of active and receptive music therapy methods with 20 participants with a major depressive disorder or a schizophrenia-spectrum psychotic disorder (Lotter & van Staden, 2019). Recordings were analyzed for themes. Findings support music as a therapy to help individuals connect with themselves and others, increase motivation, address difficult situations, express emotions, and release their energy, spontaneity, and resilience.

Art Therapy

Art therapy, as it sounds, is the creation of art. As therapy, this targets individuals with trauma, illness, and those seeking recovery. We have witnessed the powerful impacts of art, give someone a box of crayons and a big sheet of white paper and ask them to draw something that represents how they are feeling. In other cases, we have witnessed the therapeutic effects of beading, sewing, painting, storytelling, videography, photography, medicinal plant preparation, embroidery, and drum making. All of these are various forms of art therapy. Researchers promote art therapy in treatment settings for its ability to promote emotional expression, encourage spiritual recovery, and illicit creative expression (Holt & Kaiser, 2009). Holt and colleagues created the First Step Series as an approach to implementing art therapy based on Prochaska's stages of change model (Prochaska & DiClemente, 1983; Prochaska & Velicer, 1997). Using principles of motivational interviewing and the stages of change, Holt and colleagues asked clients to draw images of certain life events that brought them to treatment, for example, draw the crisis that brought you to treatment (this might be asked during the first session) (2009). Another art exercise is asking clients to draw a bridge between where they have been and where they want to be in relation to their recovery. A final example is to ask clients to create a cost-benefits collage that asks them to explore the costs and benefits of staying as they are or moving toward change and recovery. Other research suggests that art therapy is beneficial for individuals in recovery from physical and psychological illnesses (Sharp, n.d.).

Drumming Therapy

Many view **drumming** as a pathway toward healing, and a way to connect and build community. Some believe that the drum is the heartbeat of the community or nation. An evaluation of drumming with American Indian populations showed the positive effects of drumming on spirit, mood, education, and community connections. Dickerson and colleagues write about one participant's experiences, "… I felt like I was equal in the spirit, of everybody. They were taking time out of their lives, I was too, so we had consensus right there, and we're sitting around the drum and that's why the spirit works when we're all together."

Complementary Alternative Medicine (CAM)

Complementary Alternative Medicine (CAM) is increasingly being used to promote recovery and address chronic pain conditions typically treated with opioids (Urban, 2016). CAM may include massage, chiropractic treatment, acupuncture, meditation, herbs and supplements, and other approaches.

Allyson: We just completed a 12-month evaluation of CAM sessions in partnership with one recovery program located in the Rocky Mountain Region of the US. CAM sessions included massage, acupuncture, and chiropractic sessions. These were available at no cost to the participant, by appointment, at two locations. We recruited individuals with opioid use disorder, individuals at risk for opioid use disorder, and other people in the community with chronic pain conditions. Surveys assessed self-reported impacts, reasons for attending CAM sessions, and mental, physical, spiritual, and emotional health before and after CAM sessions. A total of forty participants completed the survey between March 2021 and March 2022. The evaluation found a significant increase in self-reported health ratings: physical, spiritual, emotional, and mental. The greatest increase observed was for physical health. CAM sessions positively impacted participants, 83% felt more hopeful about their overall health and wellness. The holistic CAM approach demonstrated positive impacts on overall wellness, belonging, and recovery.

Integrative Approaches

Integrative approaches that include spirituality help individuals on their recovery journey. These approaches may cognitive behavioral therapies, peer recovery support, mindfulness, dialectical behavior therapy, trauma treatment, wellness treatments, and family work. Wellness strategies could include exercise, sleep hygiene, prayer, meditation, nutrition, and mind-body techniques. Family efforts include education, groups, family therapy, and specific interventions when appropriate (Atkins, 2018). There are many reasons why people leave the healing path or get stuck on the path, this tells us that integrative approaches may be required to heal. It is never just one thing.

We Think We Are Recovered, What Now?

This is a lot to take in. The main message from this chapter is that recovery has many definitions, it is influenced by multiple factors, both internal and external, and recovery is possible, but it is not just a one-time event. We might think we are recovered. But, recovery is a process, it is walking on a healing path and starting the day with intention, prayer, connection, and faith in a higher power. Recovery is also about advocating for yourself, your family, and your community to access the resources and treatments necessary for healing.

Resources

Recovery and Recovery Support

Substance Abuse and Mental Health Services Administration, 2022 This website includes information about recovery, treatment, behavioral health services, crisis care, and recovery support. https://www.samhsa.gov/find-help/recovery

Breathing Under Water, Spirituality and the 12 Steps

Richard Rohr, Franciscan Media, 2021. https://www.amazon.com/Breathing-Under-Water-Spirituality-Twelve/dp/1632533804/ref=pd_lpo_1?pd_rd_i=1632533804&psc=1

References

Alcoholics Anonymous. (2016). 12 Steps. Available from: https://www.aa.org/the-twelve-steps

Ashford, R. D., Bergman, B. G., Kelly, J. F., & Curtis, B. (2020). Systematic review: Digital recovery support services used to support substance use disorder recovery. *Human Behavior and Emerging Technologies, 2*(1), 18–32. https://doi.org/10.1002/hbe2.148

Atkins, C. (2018). *Opioid use disorders: A holistic guide to assessment, treatment, and recovery.* PESI. http://ebookcentral.proquest.com/lib/uncg/detail.action?docID=6253999

Bergman, B. G., Greene, M. C., Hoeppner, B. B., & Kelly, J. F. (2018). Expanding the reach of alcohol and other drug services: Prevalence and correlates of US adult engagement with online technology to address substance problems. *Addictive Behaviors, 87,* 74–81. https://doi.org/10.1016/j.addbeh.2018.06.018

Borkman, T. J., Kaskutas, L. A., Room, J., Bryan, K., & Barrows, D. (1998). An historical and developmental analysis of social model programs. *Journal of Substance Abuse Treatment, 15*(1), 7–17.

Brown, A. M., McDaniel, J. M., Austin, K. L., & Ashford, R. D. (2019). Developing the spirituality in recovery framework: The function of spirituality in 12-step substance use disorder recovery. *Journal of Humanistic Psychology,* 0022167819871742. https://doi.org/10.1177/0022167819871742

Cole, D. M., Thomas, D. M., Field, K., Wool, A., Lipiner, T., Massenberg, N., & Guthrie, B. J. (2018). The 21st century cures act implications for the reduction of racial health disparities in the US criminal justice system: A public health approach. *Journal of Racial and Ethnic Health Disparities, 5,* 885–893.

Corrigan, P. W., Larson, J. E., Smelson, D., & Andra, M. (2019). Recovery, peer support and confrontation in services for people with mental illness and/or substance use disorder. *The British Journal of Psychiatry: The Journal of Mental Science, 214*(3), 130–132. https://doi.org/10.1192/bjp.2018.242

Dell, N. A., Long, C., & Mancini, M. A. (2021). Models of mental health recovery: An overview of systematic reviews and qualitative meta-syntheses. *Psychiatric Rehabilitation Journal, 44*(3), 238–253. https://doi.org/10.1037/prj0000444

Galanter, M. (2007). Spirituality and recovery in 12-step programs: An empirical model. *Journal of Substance Abuse Treatment, 33*(3), 265–272.

Garland, E. L., Manusov, E. G., Froeliger, B., Kelly, A., Williams, J. M., & Howard, M. O. (2014). Mindfulness-oriented recovery enhancement for chronic pain and prescription opioid misuse: Results from an early stage randomized controlled trial. *Journal of Consulting and Clinical Psychology, 82*(3), 448–459. https://doi.org/https://doi.org/10.1037/a0035798

Holt, E., & Kaiser, D. H. (2009). The first step series: Art therapy for early substance abuse treatment. *The Arts in Psychotherapy, 36*(4), 245–250. https://doi.org/10.1016/j.aip.2009.05.004

Jason, L. A., Guerrero, M., Lynch, G., Stevens, E., Salomon-Amend, M., & Light, J. M. (2021). Recovery home networks as social capital. *Journal of Community Psychology, 48*, 645–657. https://doi.org/10.1002/jcop.22277

Kelley, A. (2022). *Treatment program evaluation: Public health perspectives on mental health and substance use disorders.* (Vol. 1). Routledge.

Kelley, A., Steinberg, R., McCoy, T. P., Pack, R., & Pepion, L. (2021). Exploring recovery: Findings from a six-year evaluation of an American Indian peer recovery support program. *Drug and Alcohol Dependence, 221*, 108559. https://doi.org/10.1016/j.drugalcdep.2021.108559

Kemppainen, D., Kopera-Frye, K., & Woodard, J. (2008). 14. The medicine wheel: A versatile tool for promoting positive change in diverse contexts. *Collected Essays on Learning and Teaching, 1*, 80–84.

Kennedy, E. S. E., & Horton, S. (2011). "Everything that I thought that they would be, they weren't:" Family systems as support and impediment to recovery. *Social Science & Medicine (1982), 73*(8), 1222–1229. https://doi.org/10.1016/j.socscimed.2011.07.006

Lotter, C., & van Staden, W. (2019). Verbal affordances of active and receptive music therapy methods in major depressive disorder and schizophrenia-spectrum disorder. *The Arts in Psychotherapy, 64*, 59–68. https://doi.org/10.1016/j.aip.2018.12.002

McDonnell, A., MacNeill, C., Chapman, B., Gilbertson, N., Reinhardt, M., & Carreiro, S. (2021). Leveraging digital tools to support recovery from substance use disorder during the COVID-19 pandemic response. *Journal of Substance Abuse Treatment, 124*, 108226. https://doi.org/10.1016/j.jsat.2020.108226

Melemis, S. M. (2015). Relapse prevention and the five rules of recovery. *The Yale Journal of Biology and Medicine, 88*(3), 325–332. https://www.ncbi.nlm.nih.gov/pmc/articles/PMC4553654/

Mericle, A. A. (2014). The role of social networks in recovery from alcohol and drug abuse. *The American Journal of Drug and Alcohol Abuse, 40*(3), 179–180. https://doi.org/10.3109/00952990.2013.875553

Miskelly, E. (2018). *Restoration: A Wesleyan model of recovery* (pp. 1–131). Duke University Divinity School. https://dukespace.lib.duke.edu/dspace/bitstream/handle/10161/20188/Miskelly_divinity.duke_0066A_10093.pdf

Moore, D., & Coyhis, D. (2010). The multicultural wellbriety peer recovery support program: Two decades of community-based recovery. *Alcoholism Treatment Quarterly, 28*(3), 273–292. 10.1080/07347324.2010.488530

Mowbray, O., Quinn, A., & Cranford, J. (2014). *Orion Mowbray, Adam Quinn & James A. Cranford (2014) Social networks and alcohol use disorders: Findings from a nationally representative sample, The American Journal of Drug and Alcohol Abuse, 40*(3), 181–186. https://doi.org/10.3109/00952990.2013.860984

Owens, M. D., & McCrady, B. S. (2014). The role of the social environment in alcohol or drug relapse of probationers recently released from jail. *Addictive Disorders & Their Treatment, 13*(4), 179–189. https://doi.org/10.1097/ADT.0000000000000039

Oxford House. (n.d.). The purpose and structure of Oxford House. Available from: https://oxfordhouse.org/purpose_and_structure

Polcin, D. L., Korcha, R. A., Bond, J., & Galloway, G. (2010). Sober living houses for alcohol and drug dependence: 18-month outcomes. *Journal of Substance Abuse Treatment, 38*(4), 356–365.

Prochaska, J. O., & DiClemente, C. C. (1983). Stages and processes of self-change of smoking: Toward an integrative model of change. *Journal of Consulting and Clinical Psychology, 51*(3), 390–395. https://doi.org/10.1037/0022-006X.51.3.390

Prochaska, J. O., & Velicer, W. F. (1997). The transtheoretical model of health behavior change. *American Journal of Health Promotion: AJHP, 12*(1), 38–48. https://doi.org/10.4278/0890-1171-12.1.38

Rohr, R. (2021). *Breathing under water.* Franciscan Media.

Rohr, R. (2022, June 25). *Emotional sobriety.* https://cac.org/daily-meditations/emotional-sobriety-weekly-summary-2022-06-25/

Sharp, M. (n.d.). *Art therapy and the recovery process: A literature Review.* 40.

Substance Abuse and Mental Health Services Administration (n.d.). *Ten Guiding Principles of Recovery.pdf.* Retrieved August 5, 2022, from https://www.dshs.wa.gov/sites/default/files/ALTSA/stakeholders/documents/duals/toolkit/Ten%20Guiding%20Principles%20of%20Recovery.pdf

Sussman, S. (2010). A review of alcoholics anonymous/ narcotics anonymous programs for teens. *Evaluation & the Health Professions, 33*(1) 26–55.

Smith, A. (2019). *The case for keeping your recovery off social media.* (n.d.). Recovery.Org. Retrieved November 13, 2021, from https://www.recovery.org/pro/articles/the-case-for-keeping-your-recovery-off-social-media/

Urban, L. A. (2016). Alternative treatments. In A. M. Matthews & J. C. Fellers (Eds.), *Treating comorbid opioid use disorder in chronic pain* (pp. 25–33). Springer International Publishing. https://doi.org/10.1007/978-3-319-29863-4_3

Volkow, N. D., Poznyak, V., Saxena, S., & Gerra, G. (2017). Drug use disorders: Impact of a public health rather than a criminal justice approach. *World Psychiatry, 16*(2), 213–214. 10.1002/wps.20428

White Bison. (n.d.). *The Medicine Wheel and 12 Steps for Men.* https://whitebison.org/

White, W. L., & Kurtz, E. (2008). Twelve defining moments in the history of alcoholics anonymous. In L. A. Kaskutas & M. Galanter (Eds.), *Recent developments in alcoholism* (Vol. 18, pp. 37–57). Springer New York. https://doi.org/10.1007/978-0-387-77725-2_3

Chapter 5

Healing

You don't need to be perfect,
You just need to be,
Be grounded,
Be aware,
Be calm, and
Be grateful.

Allyson: How do you feel about your own path through healing? What are the anchors that you have that allow stability and flexibility in how you respond? This is definitely part of enduring well.

Dee: I work on good thoughts. My foundational anchors are grace, gratitude, generosity, joy, and laughter. These are words I embrace and repeat daily. It is a standard that I reach for each day but may not always achieve.

Allyson: Every morning I wake up, and I walk on the healing path, sometimes I am starting over, at the beginning of the path. In this book, we talk about a healing path and walking on that healing path. There have been countless times writing this book that I have felt completely unworthy and unqualified to write about healing. You reminded me that this is the reason that I can write this book, because I am still on the path. When we think about healing as a process, what does it look like? And how do we know that we are on the healing path?

Dee: Many times, individuals may think they are not qualified to offer their perception on life experiences because they failed at some aspect such as divorce, estranged family relationships, not having children, etc. In reality, individuals can have insights and understandings from "lived experiences." Because you are not healed is the reason that you can write this. You got to start the fire sometime. The tree has to grow before you can chop it down to make a fire. You cannot just say I am going to get here. Christ was on the cross. This is the tree of life. It was two beams, but it was a tree at one time.

DOI: 10.4324/9781003274018-5

Allyson: I want to talk about broken spirits and healing. How is healing the spirit any different than healing a physical wound?

Dee: When there is emotional hurt, it does impact the spirit. Just as a major diagnosis of a physical condition would also impact the Spirit. Healing of the spirit is different from the healing of a physical wound. It is not even healing of the spirit. I think what it is redefining experiences. This is how healing occurs in the spirit and the mind.

It is not a goal. Healing is a process. How do we allow ourselves to have a sense of being knowing that there is a past and a future? I think about a food processor, agitating, food mixed up. It is the presence of being able to allow the sense of being and acceptance. It is that gratitude. We are not perfect but we don't have to say that. We are who we can be right now, with the willingness to be challenged and grow. My metaphor for the house. As humans we have resources. We utilize those resources. Sometimes we have to take a break. That helps with renewal. We sleep we are renewed. We relieve ourselves which helps with toxicity. It allows us to be present and also move forward. The analogy of the house is that I have used up my resources, but not all of them. So now I am doing little things. I am going to get it finished by doing it a little at a time. I knew I needed new gates. Rather than redoing the entire fence, I am just doing the gates. When we think we have exhausted a lot of our resources, we have to ask what we can do that is manageable right now. Let's take that one walk, take that one class, have that one phone call. The capacity to say that this is manageable. Being able to reinforce that understanding. We have the capacity to do something with smaller resources towards that bigger goal if we are okay if we don't accomplish that bigger goal yet. I am never going to graduate with my degree ... bemoaning the fact that I am not getting this right now.

We can read. We can still write. We can still do. It took me 14 years to get my undergraduate degree. I did a little at a time. It took me 7 years to get my Ph.D. How do we manage these things we are moving toward? Not ruminate or fall off the accomplishment of being here right now.

Allyson: So, if healing is not a goal but a process, does that mean that we are never really healed, that there will always be things that come up, that take us away from the healing path or the goals that we have for our lives?

Dee: When we have a goal and we don't finish it how do we shift our thinking to say it is okay? John, my husband, and I had a vision about how we would live together and grow old together. He has been gone for 14 years. I buried myself for three years. How do we climb out of that? What is it that allows us to sit in that for a while? The goals shift. We are not going to be a happily married couple, but what else is there?

Allyson: So, grief and loss are part of healing, and understanding that it is okay to sit with the feelings that come from grief and loss, is huge. It is always okay to feel things; give yourself permission to feel, cry, and scream. I remember you telling me that our tears our evidence of our hearts. They represent our goodness and ability to feel deeply. Tears can be so healing. Let's talk about God. I have met many people in my work, who hate God, they do not believe in God, and that is okay. But where is this hate coming from?

Dee: You know, many American Indians associate colonization with God. And this resulted in hatred toward God; although colonization was not God, it was the White man's interpretation of the bible.

Honor and Healing

Allyson: Let's talk about honor and what that really means and how it impacts our ability to heal. Many of us have lost our honor. Our honor has been replaced with shame and guilt.

Dee: We are honor based society we had in our capacity to bring honor into our relationships by the naming, by acknowledgments, by gift giving, by the songs, by the prayers, by recognition, by being able to bring forth some kind of story as part of that honor and that shame has become such a big part of our lives that shame now is that pathway to adulthood, rather than honor the way that it was established initially. I know, growing up my great-grandmother would have us, and she would introduce us as her grandchildren, and somebody would say, "It's really good that you're taking care of your grandmother; here's a nickel." And so that little bit of recognition that little bit of honor was common, every little effort they'll say, "Your grandmother told me that you go and get water for her, or your grandmother told me that you ironed her skirt." And it wasn't that, oh, because you told me this that I honor you, it is because you did this for someone else that I recognize it and I honor your efforts. And that process and that little recognition were commonplace. So, it may not have been a daily thing, but it was commonplace. And so, the opportunity to be recognized by a small task to the opportunity to be recognized for much greater tasks. So, now I think that brokenness that we see and recognize in others is that a pathway now that we're taking that doesn't have a counterpart in honor. So now it's not that honor is eliminated it's just that it's not that commonplace, it's not that ritual that's built into so many encounters. You know, little things like babies first laugh. I mean how, how grand is that? I mean when you really think in the big scheme of things. How grand is a baby's first glimpse of sunshine? How grand is a baby's umbilical cord? There are a lot of people that have laughter as such a big part of the world, sunshine is immense across the world right now, but to build a story around babies' first laugh, around that first Sunbeam, that umbilical cord, that continues on. It goes for the retelling and the building on, and the expansion, and the ability to, create that connection between the person that does the first laugh, the person that held that first sunbeam, the person that beaded that umbilical cord. As we think about it those are the things that brought the honor, and in and of itself, it was small, but it was built on. Now we don't have a lot of those things that are built on. And because we don't have them, then we see and feel like there's that brokenness that is so much a part of our world.

It is essential to recognize the spiritual nature of everything, not only human beings, but the world we live in and the things that are around us – water, fire, trees, plants, and animals, and we wouldn't create harm by recognizing that they're part of the spiritual connection. We wouldn't you know violate. And I think that the part is that if we understand the bigger relationship with our Creator, then we wouldn't violate other people are things, because we recognize that that that that sacred relationship.

Characteristics of Healing People and Resources

Most of us want to heal. We do not want to dwell in the darkness. Healing resources can help individuals on their healing path. Our spirit and our faith are at the heart of all healing. Optimism, self-esteem, social support, forgiveness, gratitude, prayer, discipline, and mastery are the elements that help people endure stressful events and remain on a healing path.

Optimism

Optimism is about expecting good things to happen rather than bad things. We know that optimism has physical and mental health benefits. We know from a ton of research that when individuals are optimistic about their recovery, they recover more quickly (Taylor & Stanton, 2007). Does optimism come from the heart or the mind? In Michael Singer's book *Untethered Soul*, he writes about the power of our thoughts and their direct influence on how optimistic or positive we feel about the future. You are not your thoughts; you are aware of your thoughts. You are not your emotions; you feel emotions. You are not your body; you look at it in the mirror and experience this world through its eyes and ears. You are the conscious being who is aware that you are aware of all these inner and outer things (Singer, 2007).

Self-Esteem

Self-esteem is about what you think of yourself, your value, and how confident and proud you are. We know that individuals with healthy self-esteem are more like to take care of themselves and make better choices.

Social Support

Social support is about your connections with individuals, groups, and the community around you. Social support promotes resilience to stress, is protective against trauma-related issues, and improves health and longevity (Ozbay et al., 2007). Research has found that limited and poor social support or connections contribute to depression, obesity, physical inactivity, cancer, and other illnesses. Evidence suggests that social support is not about the number of connections that an individual has, it is about the quality of these connections. Similar to self-esteem, researchers often measure social support using standardized scales (Kelley et al., 2019; Zimet et al., 1988).

Forgiveness

Forgiveness and healing have been a topic of discussion for thousands of years. As an internally based process, it is a construct or idea that is grounded in psychology and philosophy. With theological and lay perspectives outlined in the Bible, the Greek word translated to forgiveness means to let go. This makes me think of the Bible verse, Jesus said, "Father forgive them, for they do not know what they are doing" in Luke 23:24. Not everyone agrees with or believes what the Bible says about forgiveness. Buddhists believe that forgiveness is about having a non-reactive mind, Hindus believe in the law of karma in previous or current lives. Both Buddhists and Hindus believe that forgiveness comes from meditative practice and understanding the illusion of self. Others view forgiveness as a coping strategy that individuals use to improve their health, decrease sympathetic nervous system responses, and foster social support (mentioned previously).

Within the 12-steps, forgiveness is an essential part of the model of addiction and recovery. Participants involved in 12-step programs create a grudge list in accordance with the principles of acceptance and surrender. This list is about writing down all hurt, anger, threats, resentments (perceived or actual) that one has. Once the list is complete, the work begins of processing and practicing forgiveness. Forgiveness has also been the focus of thousands of research studies and evidence-based treatments like 12-step facilitation therapy (mentioned previously), motivational enhancement therapy, and cognitive behavioral coping skills therapy (Tucker et al., 2015).

Allyson: We must forgive the people that we love, for everything, so that we may walk fully on a healing path. Over the years the lack of forgiveness has divided so many families and communities. I am not advocating for forgiving everyone for everything, but for those individuals we love and care about, we must forgive them. The rest … well we will see.

Dee: Yes. Forgiveness is at the core of our healing process and is a requirement on the healing path. Communities who have been offended, individuals and societies who have caused offense. You cannot have healing without an apology and seeking forgiveness. Can all of this occur without being in a relationship? For some people, it can happen on one side, so the parent or the individual with the expectation … they can forgive an ex. Or they may come to a point of healing when they lose a child or a parent. There is not a second person to have that conversation with. For the bigger picture, like social justice issues, there has to be a receiver and a giver. Harms and injustices occur in different ways. We cannot carry the burden of not forgiving others.

There is more on forgiveness in chapter 7.

Gratitude

Someone once told me that gratitude is the antidote to anxiety, and nearly everything. We know from extensive research that gratitude is the core of healing and walking on a healing path. Neuroscientists studying gratitude report that gratitude manifests in the brain, it is linked to our brain structured, social bonding, reward and stress relief, and releases a chemical called oxytocin. This chemical promotes social ties, and overall creates a sense of wellbeing, improved sleep, generosity, and lowers depression (Lindberg, 2019).

Allyson: How do you practice gratitude when life does not go as planned?

Dee: Yes. How do we shift our expectations when they will never be met? I never thought I would be a person that was alone all the time, not having a companion, but I have spent the majority or my adult life companionless. So giving up that expectation was healing. Okay this is just the way that it is. Or it could be unfulfillment. I am still mad at John, for dying. In the grand scheme of things, it is not discontent. We have to figure out how we can live in a situation where it is not expected, but it is not discontent. It is acceptance, appreciation, accepting, and gratitude. I tell myself I am fortunate every day.. life the life I have, job, flexibility, etc. I don't want for anything.

Prayer

Prayer is often viewed as a religious or meditative practice. But a 2021 Pew Research Center study reports that just 45% of adults in the US pray on a daily basis, this is a significant decrease from the 55% of adult daily prayer practices cited in a 2014 study (Smith, 2021). Researchers studying meditation (prayer) report it stabilizes blood pressure, reduces heart rate, changes levels of melatonin and serotonin, boosts immune systems, decreases stress, promotes positive moods, reduces anxiety and pain, improves self-esteem, and overall supports well-being throughout the life-span, and through the end of life (Andrade & Radhakrishnan, 2009). Prayer helps us heal (Kutz, 2004) and has many benefits for those who believe and have faith.

Discipline

Encouraging self-discipline is not just a one-time effort. Discipline or self-regulation is a gift that comes from within and it is evident by visible actions. Discipline is a long-term commitment to teaching positive ways to live in the world and to have nurturing relationships with others. Aspects of self-regulation include aspects of self-determination, self-expression, self-discipline, self-awareness, self-assessment, and self-reflection.

Mastery

Mastery is about reconnecting the broken strands of life and recreating a story, a healing and uplifting one.

Personal control or **mastery** is when a person feels able to control or influence the outcomes of a certain event or situation. Multiple studies demonstrate the powerful psychological health benefits of mastery and well-being. We have used the Gathering of Native Americans (GONA) curriculum to build belonging, mastery, interdependence, and generosity in individuals and communities (Substance Abuse and Mental Health Services Administration, 2016). Over the years we have witnessed the powerful impacts of GONA and transformation, from trauma, unresolved grief and loss, anger, and substance use, within individuals and communities. While we believe that all of the GONA principles are worthy, we want to focus on the theme of mastery. Here are some practical ways that we can practice mastery on a healing path.

- New accomplishments
- Skill building
- Practice
- Self-talk
- Confidence

Allyson: Mastery keeps on showing up on the healing path. We use that term all of the time in our work, and we've mentioned in this book. I think of mastery as having something under control, managed, and practiced. Can you give me an example of mastery from your clinical work?

Dee: There was a 9-year-old that attended treatment. Through treatment, the mother learned a lot. As they came to successfully complete the treatment, they decided they wanted to do community healing. They wrote poetry, did a video, hosted a community dinner, shared uplifting messages and affirmations, and told their story of healing. Two years later, something happened to the little girl, she was 11 then. The mother was concerned about what happened on the bus. So, the mom took the girl back to therapy again. The therapist said, "Do you know why you are here?" She said, "Yes, there was an incident on the bus. But it is not presenting a problem for me because I know how to think, feel, and what I need to do but all of those kids on the bus need therapy." This is an example of mastery.

Allyson: In terms of mastery, it is how we identify what we need? Sometimes I don't even know what it is I need to master.

Dee: The first step is identifying the need. Paying attention to our thoughts. What are we thinking? What is the story that we are telling ourselves, that we need? Once we know what we need, we can ask for that particular kind of help. With substance use disorders, many people think that it will not hurt, to just drink or use one time. Can they master that rationale? Well, I deserve to drink because of the way I am being treated. Can they master the fact they are making that decision? I am just having a good time; I can be a social drinker. Can they master the understanding that if they turn 35 years old and they are still doing that, then they are probably an alcoholic? People justify their behaviors.

Mastery can be both good and bad. With Mastery in Gathering of Native Americans (GONA), you are going to do things ... being able to choose to do good things for yourself. Mastery comes in line with a fuller you. More healthier you. Mastery is about being more in control of what makes you a better person or a healthier person, you are not mastering things when you rationalize.

Allyson: How does ceremony tie back to mastery? Tell me about ceremony and healing. I want to know.

Dee: Ceremony can be formal or informal, be all community encompassing or performed individually, quietly, and privately. The lessons and insights gained from participating in ceremonies can be described by others but only taught through personal experience. The preparation for a ceremony doesn't begin when the ceremony official begins but can be days, months, and even years before the actual observance occurs. It is important to understand that ceremonies do not function like a numeral equation or chemical mixture. The act of a ceremony in and of itself cannot bring the desired result without the personal preparation they require and following self-reflection in the days and seasons that follow. It has been taught that all ceremonies were given to us by the Creator and Spirits to be used only to benefit the people as the Creator and Spirits directed and as the People requested. This sacred knowledge that is used to perform ceremony by Holy People and gained by the individuals or families participating is never to be used to as a tool of manipulation, self-aggrandizement, or punishment but only to up-lift, to connect, and re-establish one's natural place in the Land, on the earth, and in the Universe.

Allyson: While writing this book we asked for healing stories. We wanted to share examples of how people have healed, what they have overcome, and where they are at now. Mayra Perez is someone I met while doing some work at a university. She wrote this story about her childhood, experiencing racism and discrimination at school, and how this experienced influenced her walk on a healing path. Forgiveness, gratitude, discipline, and mastery ... they are all part of the following story.

Dream: A Healing Story

Our good friend is a first-generation Hispanic woman. Her parents emigrated from a Pueblo named Matachi, Chihuahua. She received her Master's degree in Social Work, with a clinical concentration, in 2020. Growing up she had always been told that she would never graduate college due to her parents being from Mexico.

She still recalls the day that her middle school teacher Ms. Garcia (not her real name) had pulled her aside after class to ask her about her family's upbringing. Ms. Garcia commented to her that she would never graduate from college because her parents were both Mexican and her first language was Spanish. Ms. Garcia recommended she not put as much effort into her education because she wouldn't be successful. Walking out of the classroom she was sad to think that her dream of one day having a career could be determined due to her upbringing. She always remembered Ms. Garcia's words and became determined to work hard to make something of her life.

Ms. Garcia did not know that her parents worked hard to provide their children with a better future. Her dad would work at five in the morning and would get out at 4 PM. Her mother would go to work at 4 PM and would get out at 1 AM. She soon became responsible for ensuring that her three younger siblings were fed and assisted with their homework. Every time she had doubts about whether or not she should continue with school she would remember Ms. Garcia's words, following the thoughts of her parents going to work and their words of encouragement.

High school graduation came around and she could not be more thrilled and excited to know that her hard work had paid off. Ms. Garcia was the first person to receive a letter of invitation to the graduation ceremony. She continued to get a higher education. She applied and was accepted to the university. The challenge had just begun, although she had not attended one of the best high schools she realized that her high school had not prepared her to succeed in her college courses. She attended tutoring and was not afraid to ask questions in her classes to ensure that she understood the material. She was able to obtain two bachelor's degrees in Biology and Psychology. Once again Ms. Garcia received an invitation to the graduation ceremony.

Our friends passion to help people only grew as she was now working for the Department of Family and Community Medicine. She then decided to get a Master's in Social Work to continue to help by advocating and encouraging those who may need her help. She has worked with multiple community-based programs aimed at engaging and serving underserved populations. She also used Ms. Garcia's negative comments to be a driver and leader. As she continues to work with people, Mayra always assures herself to affirm people's strengths.

Theories and Research on Healing

The problem with most theories is that they are based on deficits, what is wrong or broken, and what needs to be fixed. If theories were to focus on healing or wholeness, we would know a lot more about what it takes to heal. With this problem in mind, here are some theories that are often used in the healing process and in clinical settings. As you can imagine, there are an infinite number of theories, these are the ones we think are most relevant. **Stress and coping theory** show us that how we think about stressful situations are important indicators of the coping process. People deal with stress by coping, and there are different coping responses. **Problem-focused coping** attempts to solve problems or change the situation causing the stressful event. **Emotion-focused coping** occurs when an individual tries to control their emotions to a certain stressor through positive thoughts, mindfulness exercises, or grounding. **Meaning-focused coping** is when we try to find purpose in the stressor. **Religious and spiritual coping** involves beliefs and practices as they relate to God or that which is sacred (Worthington & Sandage, 2016). **Attachment Theory** and the **Psychology of Religion**. Attachment-based approaches such as those developed by Kirkpatrick (1992) are based on the belief that the God of the universe supports the idea of a secure attachment figure, a source of comfort, and a source of safety for individuals (Kirkpatrick, 1992). This same theory has been used to explore how spouses deal with the death of a child, and how God helps individuals, and couples navigate difficult and stressful situations. The **outsider-within perspective** (1998) uses the term to describe social locations or border spaces occupied by groups of unequal power (Collins, 1998). Individuals gain or lose identities as 'outsiders within' by their placement in these social locations. Outsiders within spaces are riddled with contradictions" (p. 5) (Collins, 1998). The healing path is difficult to find and maintain when power is unequal and unjust. But everyone can heal. Teachers, clinicians, pastors, parents, children, offenders, students, elders … We are reminded of this by Rachel Naomi Remen (1999) and her definition of educare, the root of the word education, means "to lead forth the hidden wholeness," the innate integrity that is in every person. There is a place where "to educate" and "to heal" mean the same thing. Educators are healers (Remen, 1999). Educators and healers both trust in the wholeness of life and in the wholeness of people. Both have come to serve humanity (p. 35). There are also what we call **meditation models**, these show relationships between a behavior or experience and an outcome. For example, satisfaction or problem-solving models focus on solutions, transformative models empower individuals to make their own decisions, and narrative models are all about practicing forgiveness.

Dee: It is essential that we are intentional and thoughtful on the healing path. We weigh options. How do our values and principles guide us? There may be several options. We explore options. In our work with kids we use the Stop Think Consider Options Pick (STOP) framework. I really believe that resilience-focused approaches work in the long term.

Allyson: Absolutely. I can see where any of these models or perspectives might work. I know that we must be intentional on the path to healing. You know I stopped drinking. This meant I had to stay away from my drinking friends. It has been about 18 months. One friend will still not accept the fact that I will not drink with her. We were talking about getting together, we live in different states. Since drinking was the prime activity of our gatherings, I actually felt like there would not be a lot to discuss or share. She kept asking me if I would have just one drink, like one or two drinks would be okay. I could not believe it.

Dee: She was undermining you. This person does not have your best heart in mind. When you encounter her or people like her you have to be very cautious.

Allyson: Yes, that is good advice. I choose who I spend my time with. I choose to forgive others, even her.

Dee: Choice is an anchor on the healing path. How do you allow people to have that choice and do what they want to do, even when it causes heartache and sorrow? Christ died so that all could be forgiven. Of you, it is required that you forgive all. For on our part, we have to forgive everything. It goes back to that belief system. Everything is forgivable. Forgiveness is part of gratitude, grace, and generosity.

Allyson: Forgiveness makes me think about relapse, falling from grace. We must forgive ourselves and others. Jake is in his mid-30s. He is a large man, tall, wide, and a smile that nearly reaches his ears. We have been working together for about a year. He is smart, committed, and passionate about recovery. Jake has been gone. He stopped showing up for our team meetings. He stopped answering emails. He went completely off the radar. Someone said, "I think he is back using again; his behaviors are consistent with someone who has relapsed." I did not believe it. I was even mad at the person who said this ... days passed and a colleague sent another email. Pray for Jake, he has seriously relapsed. He is in a bad way. Silence. Heart sinking. How could Jake relapse? And why are we not helping him like the rest of our clients? Do people not understand that employment, his job gives him purpose, it is the predictor of recovery, of wellbeing, it is the antidote to what ails us. Instead we are judging him. We have closed the door on him. He is not welcome here anymore ... people say, "He is an addict. A user. A meth head. A disappointment."

This process has made me closely examine my own recovery. If I relapsed, would I be shunned? Would the door close? How absurd is this idea that we make one choice, relapse, and then lose everything? These are the rules of many recovery and treatment centers. We must be sober, to enter, stay, teach, research, evaluate and live. We cannot give what we do not have. We must be sober to give and teach sobriety. Is that really true? What about being pitiful and star people all at once? Can we not forgive? We will all fall from grace. I've been thinking about Jake. Was it a crisis of the spirit? What broke? What happened to trigger the relapse? What can we do to get him back? To open the door? I think of the verse from Revelation 3:20 Behold, I stand at the door and knock. If anyone hears my voice and opens the door, I will come into him and eat with him, and he with me.

Dee: My son died because people harmed him. He made poor choices. People had the choice to help him but they did not. He was in an isolated area, without cell phone reception. He could not call anyone. He did not have a vehicle. So, he wrapped himself up in a blanket and hemorrhaged to death. The reason we have to forgive is that the anger would have torn us apart as a family. Forgiveness is so important because if we don't forgive it festers, it creates another level of discontent. You have to decide if you want the event to consume you or not.

A relative's dad sexually molested the younger kids. He was in an assisted living facility. He would have gone to prison if he had not been so sick. He asked if he could come home, he did not want to die away from home. They brought him home and took care of him, knowing that the grandfather sexually abused their children. He said, "I forgave my father. I took care of him."

On the healing path, we must know and be intentional about our roles and the roles of these groups

- Role of the Spiritual Group
- Role of the Community
- Role of the Family
- Role of the Individual

Dee: God is the source of wisdom, courage, and joy. We have resentment, shame of being stupid, making poor choices, getting involved in someone, allowing ourselves to be undermined, feeling like we should do something different, not knowing. You have to forgive yourself, other people, forget about things … . you have to be cautious but how do you do that when you are supposed to be gracious? How do you not feel like a fool? It is a necessary step; it cannot be a step that gets ignored. It is an all or nothing thing.

Going back to decision-making. When people are in crisis decision-making is the hardest thing to do in a thoughtful way because you go with the immediate thing. We were at the stop sign. Siren came on. We did not see anything. We almost turned, but we saw the vehicle. It became clearer about what to do, pull over to the side. When we are in a crisis, the first thought is confusion. We cannot think well, "What do I need to do?" Let's calm down and figure out what we can do. That allows better decision-making. We do things on impulse. (Figure 5.1).

Healing Path

Dee: There are different pathways to healing. This involves stopping assessing and redirecting ourselves when we are on the wrong path. On the healing path, there is contentment. How can you support people on their own path and their healing? Flowers have spirits and watering them is an offering. We are not just watering flowers because they need it. What drives our decisions? What reinforces us so that we stay on the healing path? These are chosen steps. This is the house we decided to settle in, this is the road that we took.

Principles

We are inherently good.

We believe in others.

We learn to trust first, the love.

We have the gift of
discernment, everyone.

We are spiritual beings.

We have relationships that are
important.

Grace. Generosity. Service. Gratitude

Keeps Spirit

"Enduring Well"

Helps with processing space we are in.
We are not buried in the trauma.

HEALING PATH

How do we
enrich our gifts?

**Gifts We Were
Born With**

Enthusiasm
Curiousity
Humor
Imagination
Connection
Creativity
Resilience

Trauma challenges faith

Figure 5.1 The Healing Path.

Spiritual Paths

There are different ways that we experience and access the healing path. The healing path may be through knowledge, devotion and commitment, meditation, service and giving back, or through energy work. A spiritual path of knowledge helps us recognize who we really are and why we are here on this earth. A spiritual path of devotion focuses on surrendering to God, or that which we are devoted to. **Meditation pathways** are based on our ability to manage and reflect on our thoughts and emotions through grounding and self-regulation. **Pathways of service** bring us to the idea that serving others and giving back actually helps heal and restore our spirit. **Energy pathways** are all about what we focus our time and energy on. If we are focused on unhealthy behaviors then we will likely experience them, but if our focus and energy is on being well, balanced, and whole, we can become that.

Dee: Pathways are really belief systems. What path do we believe that we are on. It does not matter what the dilemma is, the diagnosis, or encounter, the belief system allows you to move through it. Healing is ongoing, it is added upon, enriched as you walk through different experiences. Sometimes you can feel like you are walking through the same experience, like losing two husbands, getting divorced, losing your job, or house. It can feel like you have experienced this before, but you have been enriched by your healing path so that you may have the intensity of the despair and devastation, but you hold on tighter to that hope and faith. Sometimes you have to sit in the negative space until the energy of that negative space diminishes. It wasn't that I did not know that there was some healing place in the future, it is that I had to get their on my own, it is just time.

Allyson: What if you are in such a dark place, you don't think you will ever get out of it?

Dee: When people are really depressed, if they can do service for others, it makes a huge difference. A lot of people will say I don't have the energy to do anything … . And that is true. But if you can do just one small act of service then it will help emerge from the dark hole.

Allyson: As a clinician, how do you know that your patients on are a healing path? Tell me a story so that I know this.

Dee: A young man went through the Trauma-Focused Cognitive Behavioral Therapy (TF-CBT) treatment protocol and came out amazing. He was 16 when he started. He said that he never thought he would live past his 16th birthday. He was involved in gangs, and his siblings and friends had died early. He never thought he would graduate from high school, or college, or be happy. Treatment allowed him to think about safety in a different way. It was a huge leap beyond the traumatic life he had been living. He graduated from high school and he was planning to go to college. He was happy. He cried a lot in sessions. The big thing that he did not want people to know about is that he cried in sessions. Obviously, this changed his whole life, safety was a big part of his healing. He learned how to navigate situations so that he was safer. He made the decision, about how he walked, and how he dressed. If he was walking from school, he did not take the quickest way home, that is where the gang members were. He would get on a bus and go the long way around to get home. It was very deliberate on his part to avoid confrontation and the presence of gang members. He recognized that was not safe for him. Graduating high school and getting out of there fast. He mastered everything well, he found happiness and safety. This is how I knew that he was on a healing path.

Allyson: Sometimes we want people to think we are on a healing path, that we are doing well, and we are not. I think of a good friend. She struggled with addiction. She would tell me about her sobriety, being sober, how well she was doing, her 30-day coin from Alcoholics Anonymous (AA), and that she was asked to speak everywhere about her healing path, and her recovery. But she was actively using, even as she was talking about her healing path. So sometimes people convince themselves they are on a healing path, but they are not. They are not honest with themselves or others. The message from AA To Thine Own Self Be True really resonates here. Is it really about moderation in all things? Finding balance?

Dee: Yes. Think about the circle with spirit in the middle, it is about balance. You are a runner. You have mastered running, ran marathons, you get up most mornings and run. But at the same time, you may not be eating healthy, or your spiritual health may need some work. So, there is a balance on the healing path. We must understand that we are not 100 percent healed in all areas, all of the time. The question is, "How do we find peace when things are not balanced?"

I recognize there are still efforts going forward, and part of that is the contentment to know there are possibilities … we are working on this, but still have that balance.

Navigating the Healing Path

Dee: How are you navigating the healing path right now?

Allyson: This is one of the questions I think about a lot. Am I healed? No. One of the contradictions about healing is that we arrive at a healed and whole state. This is simply not the case. I am sober. I am grieving the loss of a good friend. It will be four months tomorrow and tomorrow is her 47th birthday. But there will be no celebration like years in the past or shopping for the perfect gift. Late last night the thoughts came. I did not want to feel them, alone, sad, grief, anger, anxious … my iPhone in bed which is something I rarely do. No phones in the house is our rule. But I did last night. I went virtual shopping, from rugs to new cars, to used cabinets on Craigslist. I wanted to do anything other than feel. I found a video interview with the friend, online, one I watch when I just want to hear her laugh. I watched this because I still miss her. Thinking that drinking could probably make me feel better, even if just for an hour or two, I quickly realized I had no alcohol, and there would be absolutely no point in drinking, after all this is how she died. I woke up this morning and realized I am starting on the path again today. My choice is to walk on a healing path today. To celebrate her life. To think good thoughts. To pray. To be grateful. To love. So, the healing path is a choice and it is the choices that we make or do not make every day that tells us if we are healed.

Here are two narratives or paths that I find myself walking. Not every day. But sometimes.

Abused – Emotionally. Physically. Verbally. Sexually.

Narrative – Worthless. Pitiful. Shameful. Vulnerable. Broken in spirit.

Healed – Peace. Balance. Forgiveness.

Narrative – Sovereignty of Self. Mastery of thoughts. Spirit. Resilient. Focused. In touch with the Divine.

If I were to write out my healing path, of significant events that led to a sense of brokenness or wholeness, it was through suffering I connected with the Divine, with God. I did not feel alone. And I am grateful. Many of us struggle with finding words to name our experiences and emotions. I struggled with finding the right words to connect with the experience. Brene Brown writes about this in her new book, Atlas of the Heart. Her team collected 7,000 surveys from people over five years, they found that most people can only identify with three emotions: happy, sad, or anger. But there are actually 87 emotions that we must get familiar with in our own lives, and I would add on the healing path. Brown and her team divided these emotions and experiences based on where we are at and what we are feeling. For example, when things are uncertain or too much we may feel stress, overwhelm, anxiety, worry, avoidance, excitement, dread, fear, or vulnerability (Brown, 2021). Using Brown's list as a guide, I can see emotions and experiences that connect with all of this. From shame, humiliation, hurt, hate, anger, pride, and regret these are all part of my awareness and walk on the healing path.

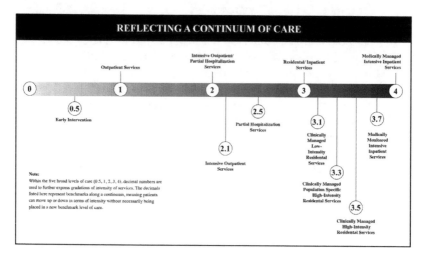

Figure 5.2 Continuum of Care.

Source: Adapted from Kelley 2022.

Treatment for Healing

Therapy helps people get on a healing path or stay moving in the right direction. In our work, we often refer to a continuum of care, Figure 5.2.

This continuum is where many people access clinical treatments and therapies. Most of these therapies require a trained and licensed clinician, and here are some treatments and research to consider. **Acceptance and Commitment Therapy** is an EB therapy model that includes, "strategies of detaching from inner experiences by relating to them differently; learning how to accept thoughts and feelings without trying to change their form or frequency; mindfulness to stay in the present moment; self-understanding to let go of concrete and inflexible thoughts or ideas about oneself; learning what is important to oneself in regard to values; and committed action and empowerment for behavioral change (Bluett et al., 2014).

Cognitive-behavioral therapy (CBT) focuses on how thoughts affect behavior and these behaviors impact emotions (Beck Institute, n.d.; Thoma et al., 2015). EB CBT practices include strategies such as learning how to delay and distract cravings by engaging in constructive activities, journaling, communicating with supportive others, going to meetings, and other positive means by which to ride out the wave of craving until it subsides. A hallmark of CBT is to address any negative thinking patterns and consider positive thinking and responses through journaling. CBT strategies also focus on thinking through the consequences of substance use and identifying elevated-risk situations. CBT may involve role-playing and be in situations where an individual learns how to navigate cravings, peer pressure, and stressful environments. CBT stresses the importance of healthy supportive interactions like peer support groups and talking circles along with physical, mental, emotional, and spiritual well-being (Worley, 2020). There is strong evidence that CBT is effective, and outcomes associated with CBT include decreases in substance use, reductions in the severity of PTSD and depressive symptoms, and reductions in trauma-associated cognitions (Curry et al., 2006; Fortuna et al., 2018). **Dialectical Behavioral Therapy (DBT)** is an EB strategy that builds skills in patients to reduce or stop use. DBT combines mindfulness, distress tolerance, self-regulation, and interpersonal development. One category of DBT is contingency management (CM). CM identifies people, places, objects, or activities that reinforce abstinence (Worley, 2020). In Chapter 4 we mentioned **Eye movement desensitization reprocessing (EMDR)** and it is worth mentioning again here because it heals trauma and more. **EMDR** is based on an adaptive information processing (AIP) model that addresses dysfunctional stored and unprocessed memories that may be the cause of a number of mental disorders, including posttraumatic stress disorder (PTSD), mood disorders, chronic pain, eating disorders, addiction, and various others (Wilson et al., 2018). **Mindfulness-based interventions (MBI)** are EB approaches that encourage individuals to experience the present moment without judgment, stress, or thinking. Research on MBI shows that it supports self-regulation, decreasing the size and activity of the amygdala which relates to worry and anxiety. Overall MBI reduces emotional reactivity and research indicates it reduces cravings for substance use (Fortuna et al., 2018; Grant et al., 2017). **Multidimensional Family Therapy (MDFT)** is a manualized, family-focused approach to treating youth with substance misuse, substance use disorder, and co-occurring mental and behavioral health problems. Outcomes associated with MDFT include reductions in problems associated with substance use, reductions in past 30-day substance use, and reductions in internalization of mental health symptoms (Liddle et al., 2018). **Pharmacotherapy** involves medications approved by the Federal Drug Administration to treat mental health or substance use disorders. Pharmacotherapy treatment depends on an individual's age and diagnosis. Often pharmacotherapy treatment is combined with psychotherapy treatment. For example, there are three medications approved by the FDA to approve opioid use disorder (OUD). These include buprenorphine, methadone, and naltrexone. A diagnosis of depression may include the FDA-approved medication of Fluoxetine, also known as Prozac.

Healing Perspectives

We are not the only ones writing about healing, recovery, and well-being. Fr. Richard Rohr writes about addiction as a spiritual disease, a disease of the soul, an illness that comes from longing, frustrated desire, and deep dissatisfaction.

Programs like AA are successful because they connect individuals to an intimate experience with God (Rohr, 2021).

Eckhart Tolle's prolific writing and speaking on awakening, the power of now, and becoming more conscious human beings is a body of literature that many can relate to. Tolle's belief is that we are beings of pure consciousness that come from God, the universal source of all life in the universe. Healing, therefore, is a process of becoming awakened spiritual beings. In this process, we detach from our physical bodies, mental narratives, and ideas, and become conscious.

Dr. Wayne Dyer's work is based on changing thought patterns that keep us from wholeness. One of the most meaningful topics that he shared with the world relates to forgiveness and love. He reminds us that forgiveness is necessary for spiritual growth, without it, we carry pain, resentment, anger, and grief that prevent us from walking on a healing path, in peace. In his 15-steps to forgiving others, one of the steps that stands out to me is switching the focus from blaming others to understanding ourselves. This is absolutely essential.

Psychotherapist, Dr. Eduardo Duran's work on healing the spirit and soul wound is perhaps the best at describing what is happening to people with addiction, and how people recover (Duran, 2006). He writes about the early stages of healing, and the importance of staying with people who can protect you from relapse, or not walking on the healing path. He recommends these ten steps for healing and walking on a healing path.

1 Pray every day for your spiritual health. Get up early and greet the morning sun with a prayer of thanksgiving. Leave an offering to the spirit of alcohol or other drugs. Also leave an offering to the spirit of recovery, wellness, and healing.
2 Meditate for at least ten minutes then do your morning routine of shower etc.
3 Breakfast should be healthy and eaten in a mindful way. Take your time and be grateful for each bite.
4 Sometimes during the day, you should do some physical exercise unless your work has plenty of it.
5 Work should be also an act of gratitude and mindfulness. Regardless of what you do for a living (of course it has to be something that is wholesome and does not hurt anyone. Sneak in a prayer every now and again if the task permits.
6 During one of the days of the week, you should set up ample time for yourself. This time can be used to see a counselor, sponsor, minister, holy person, and such.
7 Once you spend time doing spiritual counseling work then you should have time just for yourself. Treat yourself with kindness and respect.

8   With the proper motivation and intent do good things for others. These can be one-time activities or get into a project that is going to help others. Dedicate your intent to the purpose that you want to reconcile with in order to restore balance with the natural order.

9   The time with your loved ones should be part of your day. If you have a family, try to prepare and eat dinner with them.

10   Read something that is good and do some other form of entertainment before sleep. As you approach sleep, be mindful of dreams and what these may be bringing to your life. Be ready to recall your dreams and commit to trying to understand their message.

Dr. Duran encourages us to recognize that sobriety is part of living and that we are also human. Sometimes we fall short of our goals, or we walk off the healing path. We must not linger. We must keep moving forward, forgive ourselves and others, and continue to walk in a healing and mindful way.

What Now?

What steps do you follow on the healing path? Do you live in the spirit of forgiveness, gratitude, hope, and love? What stories do you tell yourself? Are you abused, victimized, not adequate? Or are you healed, fully known, forgiven, and loved? It is in the stories that we recognize the path that we are on. This is what we must remember while walking on a healing path.

Practice on the Healing Path

We recently completed a study with Native youth from around the country. We assessed their self-esteem in relation to risk behaviors using these statements, and a scale where 1 = strongly disagree and 5 = strongly agree (Kelley et al., 2022; Skye et al., 2021).

1   I smile and laugh a lot
2   I adjust well to new situations and challenges
3   I try to do my best
4   I am optimistic about my future
5   I have a sense of what life is calling me to do
6   I know that I am a good person
7   I feel that I am a success

How much do you agree with these statements? Your responses are an indicator of your self-esteem.

We measured social support in a recent research study, using these statements and the same scale mentioned before for self-esteem.

1 If I had a personal problem, I could ask someone in my family for help
2 I share my thoughts and feelings with family
3 I have friends who support me
4 I can talk about my problems with my friends

How much do you agree with these statements? Your responses are an indicator of the social support available to you.

Resources

Forgiveness

Dr. Wayne Dyer, 2011. Stanley J. Rachman, Routledge 2020.
Dr. Dyer's blog on the 15-steps to forgiveness provide explanations and guidance on how to forgive, to heal and become whole. https://www.drwaynedyer.com/blog/how-to-forgive-someone-in-15-steps/

Healing the Soul Wound and Moral Injury

Dr. Eduardo Duran, 2020. The Trauma Therapist Project interviews Dr. Eduardo Duran on healing. https://www.thetraumatherapistproject.com/podcast/podcast/eduardo-duran-phd-healing-moral-injury
The Occupational Therapist Toolbox: Stop and Think Worksheets. https://www.theottoolbox.com/stop-and-think/

References

Andrade, C., & Radhakrishnan, R. (2009). Prayer and healing: A medical and scientific perspective on randomized controlled trials. *Indian Journal of Psychiatry, 51*(4), 247–253. https://doi.org/10.4103/0019-5545.58288
Bluett, E. J., Homan, K. J., Morrison, K. L., Levin, M. E., & Twohig, M. P. (2014). Acceptance and commitment therapy for anxiety and OCD spectrum disorders: An empirical review. *Journal of Anxiety Disorders, 28*(6), 612–624.
Brown, B. (2021). *Atlas of the heart*. WorldCat.org.
Collins, P. H. (1998). It's all in the family: Intersections of gender, race, and nation. *Hypatia, 13*(3), 62–82. https://doi.org/10.1111/j.1527-2001.1998.tb01370.x
Curry, J., Rohde, P., Simons, A., Silva, S., Vitiello, B., Kratochvil, C.,..., & March, J. (2006). Predictors and moderators of acute outcome in the treatment for adolescents with depression study (TADS). *Journal of the American Academy of Child & Adolescent Psychiatry, 45*(12), 1427–1439.
Duran, E. 1949-. (2006). *Healing the soul wound: Counseling with American Indians and other native peoples*. Teachers College Press; WorldCat.org. http://catdir.loc.gov/catdir/toc/fy0609/2005046666.html
Fortuna, L. R., Porche, M. V., & Padilla, A. (2018). A treatment development study of a cognitive and mindfulness-based therapy for adolescents with co-occurring

post-traumatic stress and substance use disorder. *Psychology and Psychotherapy: Theory, Research and Practice, 91*(1), 42–62.

Grant, S., Colaiaco, B., Motala, A., Shanman, R., Booth, M., Sorbero, M., & Hempel, S. (2017). Mindfulness-based relapse prevention for substance use disorders: A systematic review and meta-analysis. *Journal of Addiction Medicine, 11*(5), 386–396.

Kelley, A., McCoy, T., Skye, M., Singer, M., Craig Rushing, S., Perkins, T., Donald, C., Rajani, K., Morgan, B., Milligan, K., Zaback, T., & Lambert, W. (2022). Psychometric evaluation of protective measures in Native STAND: A multi-site cross-sectional study of American Indian Alaska Native high school students. *PloS One, 17*(5), e0268510. WorldCat.org. https://doi.org/10.1371/journal.pone.0268510

Kelley, A., Witzel, M., & Fatupaito, B. (2019). Preventing substance use in American Indian youth: The case for social support and community connections. *Substance Use & Misuse, 54*(5), 787–795. https://doi.org/10.1080/10826084.2018.1536724

Kirkpatrick, L. A. (1992). An attachment-theory approach psychology of religion. *The International Journal for the Psychology of Religion, 2*(1), 3–28. https://doi.org/10.1207/s15327582ijpr0201_2

Kutz, R. (2004, November 1). Prayer can help with health, healing; *York Daily Record, 6.* https://www.proquest.com/docview/274464968/abstract/BADF7218A19E4434PQ/1

Liddle, H. A., Dakof, G. A., Rowe, C. L., Henderson, C., Greenbaum, P., Wang, W., & Alberga, L. (2018). Multidimensional Family Therapy as a community-based alternative to residential treatment for adolescents with substance use and co-occurring mental health disorders. *Journal of Substance Abuse Treatment, 90*, 47–56.

Lindberg, E. (2019, November 25). *Practicing gratitude can have profound health benefits, USC experts say.* USC News. https://news.usc.edu/163123/gratitude-health-research-thanksgiving-usc-experts/

Ozbay, F., Johnson, D. C., Dimoulas, E., Morgan, C. A., Charney, D., & Southwick, S. (2007). Social support and resilience to stress. *Psychiatry (Edgmont), 4*(5), 35–40. https://www.ncbi.nlm.nih.gov/pmc/articles/PMC2921311/

Remen, R. N. (1999). *Educating for mission, meaning and compassion* (The heart of learning: Spirituality in education). Tarcher/Putnam.

Rohr, R. (2021). *Breathing under water.* Franciscan Media.

Singer, M. A. '(2007). *The untethered soul: The journey beyond yourself* (Vol. 1–1 online resource: illustrations). New Harbinger Publications; WorldCat.org. http://ebook.3m.com/library/BCPL-document_id-drkqhr9

Skye, M., McCoy, T., Kelley, A., Singer, M., Rushing, S. C., Donald, C., Rajani, K., Morgan, B., Zaback, T., & Lambert, W. (2021). Effectiveness of native STAND: A five-year study of a culturally relevant sexual health intervention. *Adolescents, 1*(3), 321–334. WorldCat.org. https://doi.org/10.3390/adolescents1030024

Smith, G. A. (2021, December 14). About Three-in-Ten U.S. Adults Are Now Religiously Unaffiliated. *Pew Research Center's Religion & Public Life Project.* https://www.pewresearch.org/religion/2021/12/14/about-three-in-ten-u-s-adults-are-now-religiously-unaffiliated/

Substance Abuse and Mental Health Services Administration. (2016). *Gathering of Native Americans Fact Sheet.* 2. https://www.samhsa.gov/sites/default/files/tttac_gona_fact_sheet_1.pdf

Taylor, S. E., & Stanton, A. L. (2007). Coping resources, coping processes, and mental health. *Annual Review of Clinical Psychology, 3*(1), 377–401. https://doi.org/10.1146/annurev.clinpsy.3.022806.091520

Thoma, N., Pilecki, B., & McKay, D. (2015). Contemporary cognitive behavior therapy: A review of theory, history, and evidence. *Psychodynamic Psychiatry, 43*(3), 423–461.

Tucker, J. R., Bitman, R. L., Wade, N. G., & Cornish, M. A. (2015). Defining forgiveness: Historical roots, contemporary research, and key considerations for health outcomes. In L. Toussaint, E. Worthington, & D. R. Williams (Eds.), *Forgiveness and health: Scientific evidence and theories relating forgiveness to better health* (pp. 13–28). Springer Netherlands. https://doi.org/10.1007/978-94-017-9993-5_2

Wilson, G., Farrell, D., Barron, I., Hutchins, J., Whybrow, D., & Kiernan, M. D. (2018). The use of eye-movement desensitization reprocessing (EMDR) therapy in treating post-traumatic stress disorder—A systematic narrative review. *Frontiers in Psychology, 9,* 923.

Worthington, E., & Sandage, S. (2016). *Forgiveness and spirituality in psychotherapy: A relational approach.* American Psychological Association. https://psycnet-apa-org.libproxy.uncg.edu/PsycBOOKS/toc/14712

Zimet, G. D., Dahlem, N. W., Zimet, S. G., & Farley, G. K. (1988). The Multidimensional scale of perceived social support. *Journal of Personality Assessment, 52*(1), 30–41. WorldCat.org.

Chapter 6

Hope for Families

The Impacts of Trauma and Addiction on Families

Where are families on the healing path? Are they walking with us? Are they behind us? Are we in this alone?

Where does the Creator come into hope and healing for families? Is the relationship only between the individual and the Divine, is it more powerful when families believe and practice their faith?

What happens when families do not heal? Then what?

Beliefs About Children

In many tribal teachings, children are believed to be the center of the circle; the circle is formed by a ceremony that is made up of many relatives both in the present and those that came before them and those that will come after them. The circle is formed by the caregivers, and those who support the caregiver create the circle. Within that circle is the protection that allows for being a teacher, an understanding of purpose, a way of being connected, a way of knowing relatives, a way of belonging, a way of having an identity, a way of having a purpose, a way of recognizing boundaries and responsibilities, a way of knowing actions and learning, a way of thinking about expectations and disappointments, a means of testing and safety, a generosity of exchanges both inwardly and outwardly. This is how parents and others tend to children to help foster the self-regulation process. In this manner, self-regulation is established and reinforced.

Allyson: How do families create a healing path for themselves and their children? For example upon release from an inpatient treatment facility, or in some cases, incarceration … this is a critical time on the healing path.

Dee: There is often fearfulness, apprehension, and anxiety when family members come back. Often an enthusiastic desire for everything to be

DOI: 10.4324/9781003274018-6

well. We must determine how to help parents pace themselves with getting back into relationships with children. Many children are scared, they wonder if it's going to end in failure again. We must consider treatment plans for parents. How do facilities develop these? For example, when a parent gets a job, stable and safe housing, transportation, clothes, food, doctors' appointments ... these become part of life, but there must be a plan ... for staying on the healing path. The more these agreements are out in the open, the better understanding that the parent will have so they don't fail.

Allyson: Many families are struggling right now, trauma and addiction are driving and disrupting life. What are some words of wisdom about families and parents, what can we actually do?

Dee: It goes back to predictability, consistency, and knowing expectations within the family. When parents are honest with children, the family can continue on in a routine, and kids have predictability (food, shelter, clothing). At least one adult (grandparent, aunt, mom) provides consistency and tell children, "Your dad loves you, he makes poor choices. His poor choices affect us, but we are not going to let it affect our lives, going to school, playing baseball or having a bed to sleep on. We are not going to let this hurt us, we can pray for him, go to therapy ourselves, or see him when he is sober, we can buy him water or give him an orange drink when we see him ... but we cannot let him live with us. His poor choices would harm us more. We want to encourage him to go to treatment and stay sober." Not having animosity is an important part of this for children. We as a family can stay firm without causing additional harm to the person who is harming us.

Allyson: Oh, that is huge. Not having animosity makes me think of the importance of forgiveness. We already talked about forgiveness in Chapter 5 but it just shows up as an essential practice on the healing path. I think many families need to know that they can stand firm and love at the same time. So many families walk into the dark hole with their loved ones, and the harm then becomes pervasive and prolific. Everyone is harmed, not just the individual who was originally making poor choices. Are you comfortable talking about your own family and what this looked like? Going through this as a clinician, family member, and wife ... this gives you insight that many of us do not have.

Dee: Yes. John and I were married for almost 19 years. I don't know how much of that time he was away from us because of his drinking. When my son was about 5 years old, I was in the living room. A phone call came in. This is how the conversation went.

"Is your dad there?" ... No.
"Where is he at?" Drinking ...

"I am sorry." ... Oh, you don't have to be sorry, it is not your fault. I make good decisions.

"Are you okay?" ... Yes, I am fine.

I listened to that conversation, and after that I knew my son would be fine, even with everything we were enduring with my husband and his disease.

Allyson: What do you want kids and families to know who are going through this right now with a loved one?

Dee: It is essential that kids know it is not their fault. When kids are loved and have consistency, they can weather it better. I tried not to change our routine when John was gone. If we had something planned, he was gone, and we followed through. We talked honestly about it. Al-a-non is so important because it helps people understand that they are not responsible for the addict's behaviors.

Our Roots Run Deep

* Who are our mother trees?
* Where are they?
* What carbon (or knowledge and wisdom) has been left for their offspring (children and families)?

Allyson: I was listening to a podcast by Suzanne Simard and her work on the Mother Tree Project. This project is about finding new ways to protect the biodiversity and carbon storage of our forests as climate change impacts forest regeneration. Simard dedicated her life's work to exploring the forests, the intersection of life and history, and family within the forest. In every forest, there is a Mother Tree. The Mother Tree is the oldest tree with the most connected nodes in the forest. The Mother Tree shared excess carbon and nitrogen through networks that help seedlings or smaller trees survive. The Mother Tree communicates with the young seedlings around them and is connected to hundreds of other trees in the forests. Mother Trees can be both male and female, with both parts. Mother Trees create resilient and healthy forests, even after they pass on, they help maintain rich biodiversity. We can learn a great deal about healing and communication, final gifts, and offerings from the forests, and the Mother Tree. And our memories, genetic makeup, our relatives, and our decisions are so closely linked to the Mother Tree concept.

Dee: I love this project.

Allyson: Yes. I see the connection here. I was thinking about my family and extended family. Trauma, addiction, shame, and guilt, these are passed down from one generation to the next. A relative lived with substance use disorder and mental illness, it claimed his life at the age of 51. Another drank himself to death, he was just 54. Some view their illnesses as a moral failing. There has been a lot of shame around how they died. These relatives are part of my forest, but not the only trees, and certainly not the Mother Tree. On the healing path, we can create new stories, new forests, and new ways of thinking and feeling about our loved ones who have walked on unhealthy paths and left us too early.

Grief, Loss, and Families

Understanding trauma, loss, and death is essential.

Dee: We need to have conversations about what grief and loss mean in families and in our lives. The pandemic accelerated so many unexpected losses and deaths. All of the things that families would have encountered in a normal year were accelerated. There are different shifts in family dynamics and, now the question is, "How do we create the predictability and consistency and structure, intimacy, affection, and unity to help children feel whole again?"

Allyson: Yes, families experience grief and loss. This makes me think about the final step on the healing path, it is a transition from the physical to the spiritual world. This transition often creates a sense of loss and emptiness in families. I was just thinking about the author Byron Katie and how she encourages us to always seek truth, and the truth is not what our minds are telling us, truth is about the reality of what is, even in the transition periods of life (Katie & Mitchell, 2002). Katie watched her mother die from pancreatic cancer, she held her and looked deeply into her eyes at the moment that breathing stopped. She talks about her mother dying from pancreatic cancer. Her mind was telling her that her mother was no longer here, but her mother's spirit was still with her.

Katie's recommendations about how to journey well through life and experience love and wholeness come down to just four basic questions. These questions can help anyone as they experience loss, suffering, or struggle to understand what true reality is, and what is an artifact of our thinking. Doing the work according to Katie involves these questions: 1) Is it true? Question your thoughts. 2) Can you absolutely know it's true? 3) How do you react when you believe the thoughts that you have? 4) What would you be without the thought? Here I apply these questions to the recent death of a good friend. 1) She is dead and no longer here; we cannot be friends anymore; I cannot talk to her. 2) Yes, I absolutely know that this is true. I spoke at her funeral. I held the urn with her ashes. 3) My reaction because I believe this thought is I feel sad, alone, disappointed, and lost. 4) Without these thoughts or reactions I feel different. I don't want to have these; I want to have love for her life, celebrate her time here, and have a life well lived. I want to continue our conversations even though she is not here on earth.

Dee: Well you can still have those conversations you know.

Allyson: Yes. And I also realize that Katie's work might be too much for some, how can we love the death of a loved one? How do we comfort people who are going through loss? This could be the loss of a spouse or loss due to a choice that we made, that took us down a path we did not want to go on. We have talked a lot about suffering. You have suffered. I have suffered. What is it that we need to know about suffering and the healing path? Does suffering really have a purpose? Tell me a story about that.

Dee: One lady lost two of her children in a fire. Someone told her that she must be a strong woman and that God has given her this burden. She said she did not want to be a strong woman. I think most would agree with her. We don't want other people's bad luck to taint us. Helping children self-regulate is important too. Being willing to answer questions and recognize emotions and the need for repetition (in terms of asking questions and having caregivers ask, what do you want to know). Kids ask questions based on limited information, so a caregiver asking what you know and what you want to ask is what needs to happen. I will answer it to the best of my ability, and if I don't know, I will go and find out.

Allyson: What is happening with families today?

Dee: We see broken families. Children orphaned. Grandparents raising grandchildren. Basic needs are never met because parents and guardians are too busy dealing with their brokenness, addiction, their failures, and disappointments. Kids are never fed, clothed, or transported to school. They are not safe, they experience abuse, trauma, and violence. These are the impacts. And just a few.

And this is something that we need to discuss and address on the healing path. Families can do these things for children:

• Create and maintain a sober environment
• Promote accountability
• Prioritize family support and connections

COVID-19

COVID-19 impacted how families manage brokenness. American Indians and Alaska Natives (AIANs) experienced greater impacts (grief and loss) from

COVID-19 than the general population (Tai et al., 2021). We recently wrote about this in our research about AIAN communities Rising Above during the COVID-19 pandemic (Kelley et al., 2022). In this publication, we present the facts, in the United States, the overall incidence of COVID-19 among AIAN persons was 3.5 times higher than non-Hispanic White persons (Hatcher, 2020), and the mortality ratio was 1.8 times higher than non-Hispanic White persons. And one of every 168 AIAN children experienced orphanhood or death of caregivers due to COVID-19 (Hillis et al., 2021). his was greater than any other racial/ethnic group in the United States. This is grief and loss.

Mass Shootings and Trauma

Gun violence has increased by 33% since 2017, and in 2021 alone there were 21,000 people in the US killed by firearms (not including suicides). As the most common cause of death among children and adolescents, firearm-related injuries are now more common in this age group than motor vehicle crashes (Ogasa, 2022). Recent and historical mass shootings at schools leave communities devastated. Francine and David Wheeler lost their son Benjamin during the Sandy Hook Elementary school shooting on December 12, 2012, in Newtown Connecticut. An active shooter carried multiple semiautomatic weapons into the school, fatally shooting 20 first graders and six teachers. Interviewed nearly a year after the tragic event, Francine and David spoke about the power of forgiveness, the need for gun control, and the extreme loss they feel. Francine feels more courageous, and David has found purpose and openness because of this tragic event. Their faith was an anchor, their church family provided relentless support, and other families that lost children in the shooting gave them hope and comfort.

Allyson:　One of the common bible verses and statements I hear in songs is beauty for ashes (Isaiah 61:3). But what does this mean? For believers of the Bible or non-believers, the message is the same, that comfort is available for those who mourn, and through mourning and despair, we can rebuild and restore our lives, families, and communities.

Families, Historical Grief and Loss, and Boarding Schools

Parents and families should consider how to talk with their children about grief and loss. These feelings may be related to the passing of a loved one, or something in the news about a mass shooting, mass graves, or other traumatic incidences.

Residential schools, also called boarding schools caused tremendous grief, loss, and death among many AIAN children, and generational trauma that has been passed down from generation to generation. The boarding school movement was led by the US government, the ethos was to save the man and kill the Indian. AIAN children were forced to attend these schools, their long hair and braids were cut short, they were forced to wear uniforms and could not speak or practice their Native languages or ceremonies. The remains of 215 children were recently found in British Columbia, Canada. These remains were from children sent to the Kamloops Indian Residential School (Hazlett, 2021).

Allyson: Within many AIAN families there is historical grief and loss around residential boarding schools you were recently interviewed about how parents can talk with their kids about trauma and loss. What did you say?

Dee: Remain calm. Take a deep breath. Think about what you want to say. Offer an apology, if you can't explain to them the way that you want to explain to them, but never apologize for your tears. Acknowledge to children that their curiosity or their question is important, and that you as a parent or as a caregiver that you want to be able to give them an answer, and you may have to work on that answer. The unique part of this is why are there graves at a school because most kids don't associate children dying at a school and being buried on the school grounds. It might be necessary to share that at one time, kids went to school, and they didn't have their moms and dads with them. Someone else took care of them, and sometimes those people didn't take care of them in a good way. Some kids got hurt, and some of those kids died. We cannot just tell our children a story and close the door. We have to address what we are doing about it today. For example, I'm working to take care of my family, the best way I can, because at one time grandparents and great grandparents didn't have a choice.

Families and Recovery

We know from Chapter 4 that families are the support system that many need to walk on a healing path, to become whole again (Kelley, 2022). Sometimes this is referred to as a **family and social recovery capital.** These are resources and relationships with family, friends, and others in recovery. Relationships are the heart of every family. Relationships create the social network and structure of how we navigate the healing path. Because we are social beings, we are constantly seeking social confirmation that our choices are in alignment with the core values and beliefs of our family or social group. Without a family or social group to identify with, many people seek external affirmations, approval, and acceptance. Consider the online platform Reddit. Users write posts, share photos and videos, and link to other sources on the internet. Seekers ask questions on anything from toxic relationships, addiction, to co-dependency (and a ton more). Social scientists and other contributors post research, ideas, concepts, and data on Reddit for the public to access, and in 2021 there were more than 52 million users daily and 430 million users monthly. But the problem with Reddit and external sources of advice created by people we are not in a relationship with is that they lack context and connection. Wouldn't it be better if we had aunties and mentors who we could ask questions about life, about the healing path and what it takes for families and individuals to heal? While not perfect in any way, mainstream churches often serve as an external source of support for families. Pastors, youth group leaders, and small group leaders may know families better, and have earned a certain level of respect and confidence that a Reddit author has not.

Walking on a healing path and reconceptualizing recovery to be more family-focused rather than individualized is the first step. Here are some of our favorite examples of incorporating families into the recovery process.

Families and the Healing Forest Concept

We mentioned the Healing Forest in Chapter 5 as one approach to recovery, but it also applies to families in healing and recovery. David More and Don Coyhis conceptualized the Healing Forest and describe the environment and conditions that people need to heal. The healing forest model recognizes that change occurs at the individual level, but this change is driven by environmental factors. They tell us that change is best supported within an environment that is seeded with the resources to support personal growth supported by active involvement in a family and healing community (Moore & Coyhis, 2010). The Healing Forest is based on the idea that if one tree in a forest is sick and removed, and brought back to health, then returned to a sick forest, the tree will become sick again. Forest could be families and extended families, or entire communities. The soil and conditions surrounding the forest must be healthy, vibrant, and nutrient-dense, feeding the roots so that every tree thrives. This is what a healthy family looks like.

Al-Anon and Alateen

For families and friends of individuals misusing alcohol and drugs, Al-Anon groups provide support by creating opportunities for individuals to share their experiences. This is similar to the 12-Step and AA formats. One of the reasons why Al-Anon is so effective is that promotes abstinence as a norm, identifies sponsors or individual role models and social networks, and provides substance-free social activities like meetings, parties, and community events. When individuals attend A-Anon meetings for six months, they report better quality of life and well-being, increased self-esteem, and decreased verbal and physical abuse (Timko et al., 2015). Al-Anon also prompted the creation of Alateen, a support group for teens who are impacted by the drug and alcohol use of a relative or someone else.

Culturally-based Prevention and Prosocial Activities

From 2014 to 2019 we evaluated a substance abuse prevention program for American Indian youth ages 12–20 and their families. We worked collaboratively with tribal prevention coordinators to identify family and tribal best practices they were using in substance abuse prevention efforts. These included:

- Creator's Game, a reservation-based practice that supports sober, positive, and culturally centered activities on a reservation
- Basketball, a reservation-based activity that supports physical health, life skills, cultural connections, healthy coping strategies, and family involvement
- Drumming, with intertribal youth and families, which increases cultural connectedness and family/peer communication

Other activities with youth and families included horseback and healing rides, run/walk events, traditional sweat lodges, Sundance, culture camps, talking circles, powwows, community "block party" gatherings, beading, sewing, and preparation of traditional foods (Kelley et al., 2017). At the end of the program, we demonstrated that participation in culture and family-based activities resulted in higher levels of social support and feelings of community connectedness when compared with youth who did not participate, both are protective factors on the healing path (Kelley et al., 2018).

Faith-based Organizations and Spiritual Practices

Religious and spiritual beliefs and practices can be anchors in the lives of families, and individuals on the healing path. One study by the Pew Research Center reported that 89% of adults living in the United States believe in a God or a universal spirit (2015). Researchers at the University of North Texas conducted a review of 97 studies with 7,181 patients that examined religious and spiritual beliefs. Their review found that when patients received psychotherapy with relationship and spiritual approaches, their psychological distress decreased, and their spiritual well-being improved more than patients who did not receive religious and spiritual components (Captari et al., 2018). This finding along with many other studies makes the case for religious and spiritual involvement in the healing of individuals and families.

Researchers conducted a study of 169 African American churches in the Los Angeles area, they wanted to know how churches help individuals with alcohol and other drug use problems. Churches provided spiritual support to families and individuals linking them to referrals and providers. In more than half of the cases, family members went to the congregation and asked for help for their loved ones (Wong et al., 2018).

Allyson: My church had an old yellow school bus and drove around the town picking up kids without parents involved in the church. I recall getting to the church early so that I could ride the bus, cruise the town, and see all of the kids stepping onto the bus for some teachings about God. Our family also picked up kids in the station wagon on the way to church. Many of these kids lived in poverty, with limited family support. There were two girls living in a trailer down by the river. We stopped to get them one Sunday but they were not ready. My mom went up to the door and stepped into the trailer. The 9-year old girl was trying to find some clothes for her 4-year old sister to wear to church. There were no clothes and there was no food, the parents had not been there for a while. Faith-based organizations and people who belong these organizations can go a long way in supporting families in need. Many of these families are in crisis, experiencing substance use disorders, trauma, poverty, and poor mental health.

Celebrate Recovery

Celebrate Recovery is a Biblical program that helps individuals and families overcome addiction and trauma and walk on a healing path. It is based on six guiding principles.

1   Based on God's Word, the Bible
2   Forward-thinking
3   Emphasizes personal responsibility
4   Emphasizes spiritual commitment to Jesus Christ and total surrender
5   Believes that we need each other to grow spiritually and emotionally
6   Addresses all types of hurts, hang-ups, and habits (Baker, 2012).

Researchers conducted a study with 10 unique Celebrate Recovery sites at community churches in the US. They found that self-efficacy (the belief we have in ourselves to succeed) is associated with spirituality, and that individuals with higher spirituality scores were less likely to abuse substances compared to individuals who had lower spirituality scores. Spirituality increases self-efficacy and this research points to why faith-based recovery programs like Celebrate Recovery are effective (Brown et al., 2013).

Healthy Boundaries and Protocols

Boundaries are necessary for families and relationships in the healing journey. You may have had personal experiences with this when your boundaries were violated. Maybe this involved a family member and their illness, or it could be something as simple as a colleague at work, who constantly oversteps and over asks-making, you feel violated and uncomfortable. No matter what the situation, these guidelines will help as you create healthy boundaries in all relationships.

- Know what your boundaries are.
- Understand co-dependence and considerations that accompany unhealthy, unbalanced relationships.
- Seek support from others in maintaining these boundaries.
- Understand that boundaries are often violated through manipulation and addiction/the need for the drug.
- Provided support for loved ones without violating boundaries.

Allyson: One book that taught me a lot about boundaries was Safe People, by Drs. Henry Cloud and John Townsend. Reading this made me reflect on why, historically I have been drawn to the wrong types of people. People who care nothing about my recovery and healing, those who want to see me fail, relapse, and forget the healing path.

Dee: Yes. You must be able to identify the safe people on your healing path. Safe people, places, ideas, and thoughts.

Allyson: You have a huge heart. I am always impressed with how your family extends beyond blood relatives, it is your extended families, their families, and their families. You recently invited your nephew to live with you. I know he has battled the disease of addiction for quite some time, he was released from in-patient treatment, and you invited him to stay at your home. It sounds like things went well for a while, he was working as a cook at a restaurant, but things took a turn. You asked him to leave. Tell me about that.

Dee: When he was no longer actively staying sober, I had to ask him to leave. He was drinking daily. He had hangovers every day ... and not being productive. He was not willing to abide by the rules that everyone else in the house was abiding by. The rules are ... be polite to one another, respectful, engaged, having conversations, share meals together, visit together, be responsible for those parts of the house that you have, the bed, the bathroom, and cleaning up, doing those things that show that you are attentive to your space in the world. He made a mess out of the whole house. He needed to clean up it and he was not happy with having to do that. I told him he had to leave, he was not staying sober, and he was violating the rules the house.

Allyson: So, the rules of the house serve as boundaries. These are the guidelines that you have established, and you are committed to. So, what happened next? It can be difficult to get people to leave. The entire process can be traumatic and devastating to the family and everyone involved.

Dee: He said he would leave, but he said he could not leave until he got some stuff done. I said, "How is that my problem? The thing that you need to do is walk out the door. That is not my problem. Outside of the boundaries of my property, you can exist, but you cannot exist within the boundaries of my property. Not being able to get a bus ticket is not my problem. These are not things that I am going to contribute to a solution for. I am willing to help if there is an effort to stay sober and work toward sobriety. I am not willing to do it when there is no meaningful effort. I don't want drama in my life. If there is something going on that creates drama, I want to eliminate it.

Allyson: What is going to happen to him?

Dee: I don't know.

Allyson: Do you feel bad?

Dee: No, he was making his own choices. I would hope that he would make different choices. I still care. I want good things for him. But we are not going to shift our lives to accommodate his addiction. That is one of the things that happens with families, they shift their lives to accommodate the addictions of those they are involved in. When you shift your life around when someone is not in the right state of mind to be engaged in a positive way, it is upsetting. It makes me angry. That he did not take it ... It wasn't a problem for us to have him here, but his behavior became a problem. When his behavior changed, then I did not want to be involved in that kind of behavior.

Protocols

Protocols serve as another form of boundary on the healing path and in healthy relationships. One of the unique strengths of tribal communities is their protocols for relationships and communications with in-laws and relatives. Social roles were historically filled based on tribal protocols and practices. When individual members of a tribe or community did not fill their role, or violated a traditional law or protocol, they would be punished according to tribal/community laws. The Northern Cheyenne protocol instructs us that a male does not speak to his mother-in-law.

Dee: You don't talk to your mother-in-law, you recognize those boundaries, and you don't violate them. There are also protocols with male doctors and female nurses, if you are having a procedure done that may be invasive, it is common for a nurse of the same gender as you to accompany a male doctor during the procedure.

Allyson: Yes, there are reasons for this protocol. The goal is always to build and maintain healthy relationships in our families and lives. Protocols help us do that.

Theories, Research, and Families

Research indicates that when family members take a more active role in the recovery process, individuals with addiction are more likely to attend treatment. When families are involved in treatment programs, individuals with addiction are more likely to complete treatment. One study found a 10% increase in the program completion rate for individuals with a family member involved in a seven-day family program for residential treatment (McPherson et al., 2017).

Family Systems Theory and Life Course Theory are two theories that can be used to understand how families navigate the path toward healing. **Family Systems Theory** tells us that families are complex, dynamic, and a collection of parts, places, people, and systems. According to this theory, boundaries are essential for healthy families. Boundaries include emotional, psychological, or physical separateness within families, roles, people, and places. **Life Course Theory** is a way of understanding how life experiences occur over the lifespan and lead to life or death. Life experiences within families may include traumatic experiences, stressful life events, and various social contexts. Individuals cope with these experiences based on biological, spiritual, emotional, behavioral, and social resources (Fink & Galea, 2015). This leads well-being or the lack of well-being based on how individuals cope. One example of Life Course Theory in action is Bessel van der Kolk's book about the effects of psychological trauma, The Body Keeps the Score. Individuals are affected by traumatic stress within their minds and body, and trauma experienced by one generation is often passed down to future generations. Our bodies remember. Our families remember. They do keep the score.

Doing the Work, Hope for Families

When a family member heals, everyone gets better. There is hope for individuals and families. Trauma and addiction take us away from our families. Spirituality brings us back to the family. Grace, generosity, acts of service, and gratitude come from the healing path. We use this exercise a lot in our treatment of children and families. It encourages individuals to reflect on their thoughts and feelings related to trauma. Feelings of shame, thoughts that it is my fault, and behaviors like drinking or gambling are common. In our clinical

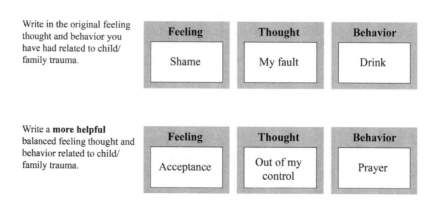

Write in the original feeling thought and behavior you have had related to child/family trauma.

Feeling	Thought	Behavior
Shame	My fault	Drink

Write a **more helpful** balanced feeling thought and behavior related to child/family trauma.

Feeling	Thought	Behavior
Acceptance	Out of my control	Prayer

Figure 6.1 Reframing Thoughts and Feelings.

work, we ask individuals and families to write more helpful thoughts and feelings related to trauma, Figure 6.1 is an example.

Allyson: I wanted to go back to when you talked about your first husband and his addiction/disease. You had the choice, it would have been probably pretty easy to join him. And that's what a lot of women do. If your husband drinks then you drink. So, tell me about that.

Dee: I don't know if I want to ha-ha. Okay, well let me close my door before I dare to reveal secrets. I think it was because I saw that it was not something that I wanted to do. I went to college and that first year it was full of freedom and all the things that a lot of kids do when they get into college for the very first time and it just didn't seem very productive. It wasn't because of meeting my husband because I didn't meet him till later, but it was really recognizing that I'm a child of my creator, and I think it was really helpful for me, that I went to Brigham Young University in Utah with the LDS church, and actually became a member of the church and there's a word of wisdom. Word of wisdom in terms of not indulging in alcohol, not harming the body and it just made so much sense to me. So, I just made a commitment that was not the life I was going to lead and I did not know when I married my first husband, that he was an alcoholic, until we had been married for a few months. I met him at BYU, and he was a member of the church and very, very funny and very strong in his belief system. And I didn't realize that there was an issue with his family and I was pretty naive to so. But what's interesting is 15 years later marrying my second husband is still being as naive and marrying an alcoholic ha-ha so the experience doesn't do very much. But I think that one of the differences between the first marriage and the second marriage is in the first marriage, I accommodated my first husband, not a lot, but when you talk about why you didn't drink with him because I think that that's part of it is, you accommodate their behaviors, because you're trying to make things right, you're trying to create consistency in your home life. And so, I think that that's one reason why spouses or partners start drinking with their partner who's either abusing substances or an alcoholic. And to have that companionship, I think there's a lot of reasons that people do that. And I think the other part you said you don't realize how destructive it can become over time. You think that things that happened to you growing up will not happen to your kids. So, a lot of times people will talk about their parents being alcoholics and how they were abused as children or sexually abused children and they don't want that to happen to their children but yet they engage in the same thing and the same thing happens to their children and then they use alcohol as a way of coping, rather than as a means of avoiding pain. And so, I think that initially there's one motivation. And then over time the motivation changes in different ways. People often realize that no matter what they do, they will never please their partner. This has to do with the Five A's, awareness and acknowledgement that we mentioned in Chapter 1.

Allyson: Do you think there is a double standard between men and women or husbands and wives? It seems like it is more acceptable for men to drink than women. Is this just part of the patriarchy or what is happening here?

Dee: Women tend to accommodate their husbands, with their drinking, whereas men who do not drink and have alcoholic wives or partners, do not accommodate them, they divorced them or separate from them, and they don't linger the way that women linger with their spouse or with their partners. And I think that that is one of the reasons why men who don't drink or stop drinking may go on to have more stable relationships, because they choose somebody that's not drinking again, or is not an alcoholic again, whereas women linger with men finally get tired of that move into another relationship with the same kind of behaviors.

Allyson: How does all of this impact the relationships that children have with their parents?

Dee: Parents may have different relationships that produce a different number of children and kids get confused about who and how they're related to … different people and what those relationships are supposed to be. At one time they may yearn for a father or a mother but then they get very angry when they realize that is not what they seem to be. What about accommodating? So many of us are born and taught to accommodate others. We put others' needs above our own. In some ways this is self-less and one of the most Christ-like things we can do, but on the other hand it can be so debilitating and overwhelming to accommodate unhealthy people in our families and relationships.

With my first husband that's what I tried to do minus the drinking, it was trying to accommodate- move where he wanted to move, do what he wanted to do, live the way he wanted to live. So, there was a lot of accommodating. And with my second husband that was not the case at all. If we were scheduling something. And my husband took off, drinking, we still went through with it, we didn't change our behavior, I mean I did for a little bit and then was like I can't do this anymore, whatever we were doing we continue to do. We didn't shift our lifestyle to accommodate his behavior. And that kind of consistency really helps children so that they're not confused and we didn't hide his alcoholism. So, it was an open discussion. And it doesn't mean that there weren't hurt feelings, there were a lot of hurt feelings. It lessened because the kids were a bit more stable. And there wasn't an accommodating syndrome. And I think there's some misconstrued kind of 'what relationships are'. For example, in dating violence or with battered women initially, it's about jealousy, I don't want you looking at another man. Partners misconstrue what jealousy is. And to have somebody love you and you love somebody else ... jealousy is something that undermines your confidence. And if you use jealousy to exert power over somebody else then that's where that broken harmful relationships get built and with boyfriends and girlfriends exploring those relationships.

Allyson: Let's talk about being honorable as individuals and in families. Can we be honorable and jealous at the same time?

Dee: When we're honorable and respectful we don't need jealousy. When there is jealousy, it undermines and brings in that shame, whether it's shame because one partner beat up the other one because they were jealous or for whatever reason. And so, we have these broken relationships that stem from people's inability to have confidence in their own love of self and it's not a selfish love. I think that what people have misconstrued, again, is selfishness and what that actually means. You know, pay attention to me only. You can't talk to anybody else, you can't have any friends, and you can't share competencies with anyone else.

What Now?

We live in a dynamic world and we are part of dynamic families, with histories and stories that extend to the beginning of time. Families often carry the impacts of trauma and addiction on their shoulders, but they do not have to.

Someone told me that we stand with thousands. Thousands of ancestors came before us, both seen and unseen. I believe this now. So the burden is not just ours to carry. This is where our faith, religion, and spiritual practices come into play. We cannot walk on the healing path for our family members, they must find it and walk on the path themselves. The most important thing that we can do is to be healthy and in balance, seek help and resources when we need them, have healthy boundaries and relationships, and do the work that we are called to do. This is what gives us hope for families and recovery.

Practice on the Healing Path

Review Figure 6.1

Write an original feeling, thought, and behavior you have had related to a child or family trauma. Our example is: feelings of shame, thoughts it is my fault, behavior is to drink.

Write a more helpful balanced feeling, thought, and behavior related to child or family trauma below the original feeling, thought, and behavior. Our example is feeling of acceptance, thought that it is out of my control, and behavior is to pray.

What is the difference? What is most helpful on the healing path?

Resources

American Academy of Child and Adolescent Psychiatry, Resources on Families and Youth, Mass Shootings, and clinical practice, https://www.aacap.org/

Boundaries by Henry Cloud and John Townsend, 2017, Zondervan, https://churchsource.com/search?q=boundaries

Choice Theory, The Classer Institute for Choice Theory, https://wglasser.com/what-is-choice-theory/

Family of Al-Anon Family Groups, https://al-anon.org/

Federal Bureau of Investigations, Active Shooter database, https://www.fbi.gov/file-repository/active-shooter-incidents-in-the-us-2021-052422.pdf/view

National Child Traumatic Stress Network (NCTSN), https://www.nctsn.org/resources/helping-children-with-traumatic-separation-or-traumatic-grief-related-to-covid-19

Safe People by Henry Cloud and John Townsend, 1995, Zondervan, https://www.zondervan.com/9780310210849/safe-people/

The Body Keeps the Score: Brain, Mind, and Body in the Healing of Trauma by Bessel van der Kolk, 2015 Penguin Books, https://www.christianbook.com/keeps-score-brain-mind-healing-trauma/bessel-van-der-kolk

The Healing Forest: A Model for Community Wellbriety by White Bison, http://peter.growinme.com/wp-content/uploads/Healing-Forest-Community.pdf

The Mother Tree Project by Suzanne Simard, https://mothertreeproject.org/about-mother-trees-in-the-forest/

References

Baker, J. (2012). *Your first step to celebrate recovery: How god can heal your life.* Zondervan.

Brown, A. E., Tonigan, J. S., Pavlik, V. N., Kosten, T. R., & Volk, R. J. (2013). Spirituality and confidence to resist substance use among celebrate recovery participants. *Journal of Religion and Health, 52*(1), 107–113. https://doi.org/10.1007/s10943-011-9456-x

Captari, L., Hook, J., Hoyt, W., Davis, D., McElroy-Heltzel, S., & Worthington, E. (2018). Integrating clients' religion and spirituality within psychotherapy: A comprehensive meta-analysis: CAPTARI et al. *Journal of Clinical Psychology, 74,* 1938–1951. https://doi.org/10.1002/jclp.22681

Fink, D. S., & Galea, S. (2015). Life course epidemiology of trauma and related psychopathology in civilian populations. *Current Psychiatry Reports, 17*(5), 31. https://doi.org/10.1007/s11920-015-0566-0

Hatcher, S. M. (2020). COVID-19 Among American Indian and Alaska Native Persons—23 States, January 31–July 3, 2020. *MMWR. Morbidity and Mortality Weekly Report, 69.* https://doi.org/10.15585/mmwr.mm6934e1

Hazlett, A. (2021, September 26). *How parents can talk to kids about residential boarding schools.* Social Good. https://sea.mashable.com/social-good/17653/how-parents-can-talk-to-kids-about-residential-schools

Hillis, S. D., Blenkinsop, A., Villaveces, A., Annor, F. B., Liburd, L., Massetti, G. M., Demissie, Z., Mercy, J. A., Nelson III, C. A., Cluver, L., Flaxman, S., Sherr, L., Donnelly, C. A., Ratmann, O., & Unwin, H. J. T. (2021). COVID-19–associated orphanhood and caregiver death in the United States. *Pediatrics, 148*(6), e2021053760. https://doi.org/10.1542/peds.2021-053760

Katie, B., & Mitchell, S. 1943-. (2002). *Loving what is: Four questions that can change your life* (1st ed., Vol. 1–1 online resource (xxvi, 258 pages)). Harmony Books; WorldCat.org. https://www.yourcloudlibrary.com

Kelley, A. (2022). *Treatment program evaluation: Public health perspectives on mental health and substance use disorders.* (Vol. 1). Routledge.

Kelley, A., Fatupaito, B., & Witzel, M. (2018). Is culturally based prevention effective? Results from a 3-year tribal substance use prevention program. *Evaluation and Program Planning, 71,* 28–35. https://doi.org/10.1016/j.evalprogplan.2018.07.001

Kelley, A., Small, C., Milligan, K., & Small, M. C. (2022). Rising above: Covid-19 Impacts to Culture-Based Programming in Four American Indian Communities. *American Indian & Alaska Native Mental Health Research: The Journal of the National Center, 29*(2), 49–62. WorldCat.org.

Kelley, A., Witzel, M., & Fatupaito, B. (2017). A review of tribal best practices in substance abuse prevention. *Journal of Ethnicity in Substance Abuse, 18,* 1–14. https://doi.org/10.1080/15332640.2017.1378952

McPherson, C., Boyne, H., & Willis, R. (2017). The role of family in residential treatment patient retention. *International Journal of Mental Health and Addiction, 15*(4), 933–941. https://doi.org/10.1007/s11469-016-9712-0

Moore, D., & Coyhis, D. (2010). The Multicultural Wellbriety Peer Recovery Support Program: Two decades of community-based recovery. *Alcoholism Treatment Quarterly, 28*(3), 273–292. https://doi.org/10.1080/07347324.2010.488530

Ogasa, N. (2022, May 26). Mass shootings and gun violence in the US are increasing. *Science News*. https://www.sciencenews.org/article/gun-violence-mass-shootings-increase-united-states-data-uvalde-buffalo

Pew Research Center (2015).U.S. public becoming less religious. *Pew Research Center's Religion & Public Life Project*. https://www.pewresearch.org/religion/2015/11/03/u-s-public-becoming-less-religious/

Tai, D. B. G., Shah, A., Doubeni, C. A., Sia, I. G., & Wieland, M. L. (2021). The disproportionate impact of COVID-19 on racial and ethnic minorities in the United States. *Clinical Infectious Diseases, 72*(4), 703–706. https://doi.org/10.1093/cid/ciaa815

Timko, C., Halvorson, M., Kong, C., & Moos, R. H. (2015). Social processes explaining the benefits of Al-Anon participation. *Psychology of Addictive Behaviors: Journal of the Society of Psychologists in Addictive Behaviors, 29*(4), 856–863. https://doi.org/10.1037/adb0000067

Wong, E. C., Derose, K. P., Litt, P., & Miles, J. N. V. (2018). Sources of care for alcohol and other drug problems: The role of the African American Church. *Journal of Religion and Health, 57*(4), 1200–1210. https://doi.org/10.1007/s10943-017-0412-2

Chapter 7

Gratitude and Enduring Well

The Invitation

We are nearing the end of this writing journey however this ending is also an invitation to take your next steps with gratitude and to endure well. What this means is the opening of opportunity for readers to embrace the ongoing journey with renewed hope, joy, and enthusiasm. We were born with curiosity and that trait probably increased for some and decreased for others. If, there has been more sadness and sorrow, then anticipating the next steps and being curious about the next phase may have dimmed. Hopefully, the prior chapters have helped to prepare for letting go with a level of mastery and confidence in the understanding of how brokenness impacts our thoughts, feelings, behaviors, and relationships. You may be wondering how this will end, the book that is. And, what we want to share with you as we make our final journey in this chapter.

When we set out to write this book, prayed about it, visioned for it, talked about it ... there was agreement that it had to include our faith and our beliefs. After all, these are anchors in our lives, our faith is how we navigate our individual and collective pathways, embracing the pathways, getting up each day, ending each day, and being in a relationship with those living things around us. But the idea that we could include concepts of faith and belief in a book on clinical and practical applications to healing was a challenge. Our publisher is not faith-based, and we are not saints, gurus, pastors, or monks. We are just two very different people with experiences on the healing path. There are four anchors or key messages that we must share with you as the final gifts, or what we have learned on this journey.

1 Healing is not a destination. We do not walk on a healing path and arrive at the end, healed. We begin each day or sometimes each minute, a bit further down the path. Sometimes we find ourselves on the wrong path.
2 Healing is not an outside job. There is nobody or no thing that can heal. Healing comes from the restoration of the mind, body, soul, and spirit. It's

DOI: 10.4324/9781003274018-7

the balance that we strive for and the self-revelation, self-awareness, self-acknowledgment, and self-understanding that comes. We look to pills, people, books, therapy, and more. These might help us, but they alone, will not heal us.

3   Healing involves service, generosity, forgiveness, and love. When we see acts of service, generosity, and love ... we see the healing path and the lives of people on that path. We can recognize the path because we are on that path too.

4   Healing is a spiritual journey. When we embrace spiritual practices, service to others, and uplifting beliefs, we find other people who are on similar paths. There is reassurance in being with others who embrace the Great Mystery and endure well.

We cannot live without contradiction on the healing path.

Our Choices

Natural laws tell us that for every choice there will be a consequence. For some individuals, there is a need for external controls, such as detention, prisons, and fines, when regulations or laws are violated. We need to have laws that are fair and equitable with most of the citizens voting and endorsing inclusion, safety, protection, and equity for the various populations across the country and the world. However, some laws take away personal autonomy because of other person's belief systems or the encroachment of religious ideation into decision-making that affects the quality of life. For women especially this is truly a violation of God's gift of choice.

Personal choice and accountability are the balms that counters traumatic experiences or brokenness. Being able to have control, decision-making capability, understand interconnection between feelings, thoughts, and responses, and making meaning of traumatic experiences is what moves individuals toward enduring well.

Dee: When others use control or other means to take away a person's choice, I believe that this person is interfering with the God given gift of choice and accountability for the other person. There are many ways this is manifested, and I think this is driven by a sense of power, greed, ownership, privilege, revenge, and self-righteous. Traits that create brokenness and contributes to trauma and dysfunction. Parents may have good intentions but when they control all aspects of their child(ren) lives, children do not learn from exploration and curiosity, but from fear and anxiety. Anxious individuals consume much fearfulness and apprehension, contributing to paranoia, conspiracy, and seeking a sense of protection and control over self and others.

Living with Contradiction

Allyson: Let's talk about Roe vs. Wade. This is a huge time in our history. I cannot believe that we have regressed to the point of taking away women's rights, the right to healthcare, and the right to choose.

Dee: Yes. It is a sad time because the first gift given to us as spirits was the right to choose. In the spirit world before we gain physical bodies, we were presented with the choice of choosing the Creator or to choose Satan. We were given the choice to come from spirits to gain physical bodies, entering into this earthly world with a body and a spirit. Our Creator presented us with the opportunity to choose Him or not. Allowing us to have the ability to choose and make decisions for ourselves. The problem is that we must have the right to choose. With everything in our lives, the choice must be available to us. We can say we do not believe in abortion, it is wrong, it is murder, and it is unethical, but none of those considerations should take away the right to choose what happens with our own bodies, hearts, minds, and spirits. What matters is that as spiritual children of a loving Heavenly Father, who presented us with choice and accountability, that we have free will and free agency and the right to choose.

Allyson: Writing and talking, we always come back to these two journeys or paths that we are constantly navigating. On one journey we endure well, become our best selves, we believe wholeheartedly that we are made of the stars, that we are star people, sacred people, we walk in beauty. On another journey we do not endure well, we are pitiful people who make bad choices, we harm others, and fail to manage life. As a person who has walked as a star person and as a pitiful person, daily, sometimes hourly, I see this as a complete contradiction.

Dee: Yes, contradiction is always present in our lives because of our choices, it actually gives us choice. If there was no contradiction, we would not have the capacity of choice. We get to choose how we are going to live our lives and to whom we will devote our lives to. We get the choice of decision-making ... when we recognize that the choice is a gift, then we are on a healing path. God wants me to be in this place or that place ... there are times when we get distinct impressions, inspiration, or revelations that we need to do things in a certain way, the choice is, "Do we want to follow that prompt or not?"

There is a contradiction. How do we live with contradiction? If you have the belief about God and Christ and Adam and Eve, one commandment was to not partake of the forbidden fruit, but the other was to multiply and have children. This is a contradiction, you had to abide by one commandment or the other, and you could not do both. The idea is that we are not to covet our neighbor's wife, yet we are supposed to be self-sufficient and take care of ourselves. How do you build this capacity unless you look at someone else to see how they did it? I think this goes back to choice and accountability. How can we have a choice if there are not two options or if there is no opposition in all things? This understanding can help provide a perspective on why bad things happen. If you believe in God, then you must believe there is opposition. For example, believers think Satan creates havoc using individuals' free will who are willing to bend toward his desires. Greed, revenge, control, human trafficking, war, privilege, selfishness, brutality, aggression, all those conditions that are man-made that contribute to harm and threat toward another is at the hands of someone exercising their free will.

Spirituality, Forgiveness, and Gratitude

It is difficult to be grateful in times of trauma, crisis, despair, and loss. Throughout this book, we have shared stories about forgiveness and gratitude on the healing path, and out of everything these two constructs seem to rise to the top, as the most essential ingredients in healing. Spirituality, religious beliefs, and practices often help us grow our capacity to love, forgive, and have gratitude for others and for ourselves (Gaventa, 2013). Research tells us that forgiveness and gratitude are character strengths that help people walk on a healing path (Breen et al., 2010). When people report higher levels of gratitude and forgiveness, they are less likely to feel lonely or depressed (Thompson et al., 2005). Individuals who practice gratitude and forgiveness also are more accepting, empathetic, and have greater self-love and compassion. Our spirituality is at the core of these two practices.

Allyson: Grace, gratitude, joy, and generosity. These are words that describe you, Dee. And they are also signs of the healing path. How do these show up in our lives?

Dee: Being grateful and being of service. So, when you think about each generation before us, every generation has prayed for the next generation and generations going forward. It certainly was the prayers of my elders and their prayers that they heard and the prayers from each generation back that said, "You do good things." Their stories about prayers of others on behalf of me and hearing my mother and grandmother pray for my children and grandchildren. When you think about it, it's not us alone. We are never alone.

Generosity – is about abundance, having a generous spirit and giving freely to others without expecting anything in return. I had the benefit of the generosity of a lot of people. I think that we have to look at it in terms of are we giving them a gift that is really usable? Or are we giving them a white elephant gift that just doesn't have a function? I think that with our exchanges, and I don't know how long it's been that we've known each other, but the gifts, giving between the two of us have been very meaningful because it's an exchange of ideas and understandings and love and generosity and respect. But take another relationship where it's not one built upon love and respect, and you have an exchange of gifts, I shouldn't call it gifts- exchange, and it's built upon deceit or deceiving and not respect. Then when you walk away from those relationships you don't want those things.

Grace – is that element of forgiveness, restitution, reconciliation, love, appreciation, and unworthiness. In spite of what we have done, everyone can have a healing journey and be worthy of that healing journey.

Gratitude – the appreciation, recognition of blessings in various ways, blessings of not recognizing the blessing, people will hope and pray for something, but they realize they received more than what they had anticipated. I think of Garth Brooks' song, Thank God for Unanswered Prayers. We can have gratitude for things we do not have. We recognize the abundance of blessings we do have and the contentment. The desire to be satisfied with what is present because there is such an expression of gratitude. The tearfulness of saying I am so blessed.

Joy – this is joy, here is a photo of my new grandbaby. And a friend had been in long-term relationship, but his partner did not want a family. He broke up that relationship. He prayed for a family. Two eagles came and flew over him. His current partner had a niece who was pregnant, she delivered twins. Those twins are now 13, that is joy.

Allyson: While writing this book we asked our friends and colleagues to write stories about healing. I was shocked at the limited response, the unwillingness to share stories. This was among healers, people who walk on a clinical healing path each day, to help others on heal from trauma and addiction. Were they not willing to share because they are not ready? They are not healed? Or is it because the process of healing is so deeply personal, it is uncomfortable to share? We received three healing stories. This story is from a mother who grieved the passing of her son and how she healed.

Dee: Healing is deeply personal.

Alcoholism, Drug Addiction Mental Illness, Suicide: Healing Is Not a Solo

When I held my newborn son in my arms, I was enveloped in an outpouring of love that I had never felt before. For three days I was on a "spiritual high." I felt love for everybody, and especially for this sweet baby. I knew Jonathan had a special mission to perform on this earth. Jonathan seemed perfect at birth. As he grew older, some disabilities surfaced. He was slow to crawl, walk, and talk. At age three, he started speech therapy because he told me, "My friends say me talk baby talk, and me do." With severe learning disabilities, Jonathan was often teased and bullied. At age 15, he started using drugs and alcohol to dull his emotional pain and fit in somewhere. "Druggies" will accept anyone into their circle. Addiction brought its debilitating companion of mental illness—depression, anxiety, paranoia, schizophrenia, and suicidal ideation. It also brought rehabs, jails, psychiatric hospitals, and homeless shelters. In my desire to help Jonathan, my son Ben and I wrote and produced a music album called, Wings of Glory: Songs of Hope and Healing from Addiction. It brought Jonathan a ray of hope, and I believe the music helped keep him alive for twenty years. At the age of thirty-five, Jonathan took his life. He had been sober for 3 years, but the cruel claw of mental illness refused to release its relentless grasp. Depression finally took him down. What had happened to my sweet baby who had been born with such promise? As I grieved, I saw Jonathan's life from a new perspective. I realized that he had accomplished his mission in an extraordinary way. When others were rude, he was kind. When others were angry, he was patient. When others were critical, he was compassionate. When others were faithless, he believed. When others were timid, he was brave. The great outpouring of love I felt at Jonathan's birth was prophetic. Jonathan's mission was to teach us how to love. Now he was gone. My healing journey began when I turned to my Savior, Jesus Christ. I knew He knew my pain, and I knew He wouldn't leave me alone in my grief. Healing is a day-by-day journey with many ups and downs and a few plateaus. Healing is not a solo. It is a duet, a trio, a quartet, or a whole chorus. To heal, you need people around you to talk to you when you're sad, to laugh with you when you're remembering the good times, to pick you up off the floor when you crumple to the ground, to sing songs of rejoicing with you when the reality of Christ's resurrection and the promise of eternal life for everyone burns in your soul. If you don't believe in Jesus Christ, believe in a "Higher Power." Believe in a magical, marvelous, miraculous way that you are going to be with your loved one again someday. As you hold that vision in your mind, you will begin to heal. – A Grieving but Healed Mother, 2022.

Suffering and Loss

Allyson: We have been doing work in communities and clinical settings for a while now. One question that always comes back to us, in one form or another is, "What is the purpose of suffering?" People and families want to know how it is possible to maintain faith and endure well when there is so much loss, grief, suffering, and tragedy in the world.

Dee: Scriptures tell us that Job did nothing wrong, it was without cause that Satan sought to destroy him (Job 2:3). Job is probably a fallback to explain unexplainable suffering, however there is much more understanding that we can bring to the conversation. Scriptures indicate, "... ... if the billowing surge against them, if the very jaws of hell shall gape open the mouth wide after thee, know thou, my son, that all these things shall give thee experiences and shall be for thy good' (Doctrine and Covenants Section 122:7). Elder Orson F. Whitney states, "There is the reason. It is for our development, our purification, our growth, our education, our advancement, that we buffet the fierce waves of sorrow and misfortune; and we shall be all the stronger and better when we have swum the flood and stand upon the farther shore" (1918).

For those who are faith-based, scriptures or prophetic understanding can help with the meaning of enduring well and embracing those traumatic events that are there for our experiences. There is a bigger conversation that can be had about spirituality, religiosity, humanity, humanistic, Christian and non-Christian beliefs, and secular and agnostic perspectives. For those who question spiritual or religious connotations, there is the understanding that there are natural laws that humanity must abide by, if natural elements are defied, there will be consequences. If one smokes, there is a high probability of lung cancer. If one lives in a toxic environment, the likelihood of dire outcomes is higher. The Adverse Childhood Experiences (ACEs) studies we mentioned in Chapter 3 remind us that when kids experience harsh living conditions during their first 18 years of life, they are more likely to experience poor mental, physical, emotional, and spiritual health as adults (Felitti et al., 1998).

In addition, there is also a Great Mystery that exists in this universe that for those who do not believe in a spiritual deity, however, there is still the acceptance that there is a spiritual element in place. Some find this through God, while others do not.

Allyson: Many people do not believe in God. There is too much suffering in the world, too many mass shootings, natural disasters, and horrific events that a God of love would certainly not allow. It is somewhat easy to create the no-god argument when evil, darkness, and despair are everywhere. Rohr writes about this; God allows and does not stop suffering. God participates in human and earth-bound suffering with us, we are not alone. It is because of this shared suffering that we can love one another and experience a connection to the Divine (Rohr, 2021). Other studies have found that most people feel there is meaning in suffering (Helming, 2011).

Dee: As we think of enduring well, God does not give us more than what we can endure ... however I think we tend to hang on the edge of that burden thinking we cannot endure more. And we struggle, suffer, and mourn on that edge. I think many times we look back and say, "How did I manage to come out on the other side of all that grief, sorrow, loss, and wretchedness?" We realize we would have to die ourselves to not endure those periods of brokenness. In sorrow. The scriptures tell us that Jesus wept. Even when we have an abundance of blessings and things that can uplift us, there are times we are going to be sorrowful. That is when we call upon our faith. Faith is not science-based. If someone is going for science to prove there is a God, that is not the way that proof comes about. I think the other part of that is the laws. We have the laws of the physical world, we can measure things according to these laws and their physicality ... but we cannot use those same measures, to measure something that is not in that realm.

Grief and Loss, and Enduring Well

Allyson: We will all experience grief and loss, and it is in the moments that we can draw on our sense of purpose, are connection to the Creator, or we become pitiful and hopeless. In my life I have done both. I have used alcohol to cope with loss and grief. It did not end well. I have also recognized that alcohol and unhealthy behaviors are not how I want to live.

Dee: This is a human condition. When does it move into jeopardizing the sense of stability a person has, in that an individual is not functioning at a level that they want? For the most part, with a supportive environment, people can move through grief and loss, even serious or complicated situations. As we think about environmental conditions and the histories we have, how do we deal with intense grief and loss? There is a black hole that is grief and loss. It gets complicated by all kinds of other things. If you don't have a support system. If you have multiple losses. If there is high vulnerability. If there are limited resources, then that makes it difficult to work through, find anchors, and to have that grounding that allows for enduring well.

For my Tribe, the Caddo's we follow these steps when a loved one passes on.

- Within four days there will be a burial
- Within one week a memorial dinner (a brushing off/cedar ceremony)
- This occurs two additional years (dinner and ceremony)

These are checks, even self-checks with self/others, where are we at and how are we doing.

There is a surrounding network of people to support you. It has been a year, but I still feel like it just happened yesterday. It's an affirmation that this is still the process. In a year or two years, you can say. I cannot believe it has been this long. I can say his name now. I can look at the photos and smile. The sadness is not as intense. It is still a huge loss but I can remember the good times. My grief is as real as anyone else's grief. But now joy is expanded beyond the grief.

It is important to think about the helpers. My husband, when he was sick, he took 28 pills every morning. He would line them up and say okay little soldiers it is time to do your work. We have to think about the purpose of things. Of ceremony. Feelings … . It is okay to feel things

With addiction, it's tolerance or wanting to feel good or escape …

Having time to reflect and get feedback is important.

Allyson:	I received a call. My dear friend passed away unexpectedly in the night. She died from alcohol poisoning. Her two children and husband found her in bed.
Dee:	Tell me about that. What happened after you received the call?
Allyson:	The day after the call I was reeling, crying, mad, hysterical, grasping for photos, and re-reading text messages and emails from 30+ years. I was wishing there was a last letter or gift in the mail from here … . A phone message or just anything that reminds me of her. But there is not. She has transitioned. Last night when I went to bed, I did not sleep. I was so disappointed because I felt like if I did sleep, she would come to me, much like my aunt did, but she has not, or at least not yet. After I learned of her passing, I started reading about what happens to the body when we die from alcohol poisoning. I had to know exactly what happened at the point of death. The research and reports are mixed from brain-stopping to breathing stopping, to a coma … but at the end of the day, it does not sound like any pain, and that gives me some solace. But I am still mad, just for today. Grief comes in waves. I think about her final journey home at 46 why did she have to make this journey so soon? We had travel plans, beach plans, and business plans. And I feel extreme guilt. Over the last few years, her drinking became worse. She would call me at all hours of the day and night. Drunk. I would not be able to understand her, and she would not remember the next morning. I started to tell her that I could not talk to her when she was drunk. She still called and texted, but it became less frequent. Today I am sitting here wondering if my actions if different would have led to a better outcome. Maybe she would be alive today if I picked up the phone. That is the question and the guilt that I will live with for a while. They called today, and want me to speak at her funeral, I don't know if I can do it, and I don't know what I will say.
Dee:	You will speak in a way that honors her life. Pick three or four anchors, things that represent her, who she was, and what you want people to know about her. Take these anchors and create stories, tell

stories that give people hope and joy, and celebrate her life. You must do this.

Allyson: I know. The stories are a good idea. I will have to think about those stories, there are many. Do I mention the disease, the addiction? Or do I just stay with the positive memories and stories?

Dee: No, you do not go to the dark hole. You will not remember her in this way. We can all go there, but we must decide whether we will not go there or stay there. It does not benefit anyone.

Allyson: You are right. It is where the mind wants to go, the pitiful place, the dark hole, but that is not how I want to remember her.

Dee: How did it go, how was the funeral, and what did you say?

Allyson: There were about 600 people in our old high school auditorium. I talked about her life, told stories, and remembered all of the joy and good times. I shared these anchors about the way that she lived so that she could be remembered with love and hope for something beyond this life on earth.

1 Family is the constant anchor in life, love them, spend time with them, and celebrate with them. This was how she lived.
2 Find out what you want and go after it. Don't stop until you have whatever that is.
3 Have fun. Laugh loud. Life is too short not to have fun.

In some ways this was the last tribute to her, it was her final send-off. I left people knowing and remembering the person that I knew. The one that lived fully and loved deeply before addiction consumed her life. It has been four months since she passed on. I have experienced most of the grief cycle and I keep going back to denial, anger, bargaining, depression, and almost acceptance. Kubler-Ross' grief cycle is my cycle. I am trying to find meaning in all of this. And, I have not found it yet.

Dee: You will. It will take time.

Allyson: I hate that we must go through the process of grief. But I realize that we do not have a choice. If we lose someone that we love, then we invariably will experience grief. How we emerge from the grief process is our choice and also the work of the Creator.

Dee: The Cheyenne's have a call-back ceremony, calling our spirits back. The Cheyenne's also have rules about dancing and speaking in public after the death of a loved one. Observing these rules and protocols is a way of staying connected to the culture, the beliefs, and the loved one who has passed on. What are the beliefs we have about death? Do we think it is final or do we think it is a door opening we cannot see with our physical eyes?

Allyson: Tell me about staying connected to our loved ones who have made their final journeys home. Your son passed away. I really enjoyed it when you talked about him with me. I have known you for 20 years, but I never knew about his life.

Dee: Yes. It is difficult to talk about him. I miss him. Well, I do not know the answer, but I can tell you what I believe and what others believe. I am a Christian, so I believe that when we die, we go to heaven. In heaven we are reunited with our loved ones, there is no pain or guilt, or addiction. Did you know Paulette Running Wolf? She died a few weeks ago. She had a passion for children and families, and all Indian people. She was in a car crash near Browning Montana. She died on the way to the hospital. I am crushed.

Allyson: I am so very sorry. What a tragic and unexpected loss.

Dee: Yes. So don't go dying on me.

Allyson: Well, I guess it was just her time to go.

Dee: No, it was not her time to go. It was the choices and decisions of other people that caused her death. God did not cause this death.

Allyson: Well, that is an interesting perspective. I've always thought that God knows the day we will be born, and the day we will pass on. This is written in the book of life. Solomon writes about life being a series of beginnings and endings, Solomon's father King David writes in Psalm 139:15–16, You watched me as I was being formed in utter seclusion, as I was woven together in the dark of the womb. You saw me before I was born. Every day of my life was recorded in your book. Every moment was laid out before a single day had passed. And this was echoed by Job in the Old Testament of the Bible tells us that God has decided the length of our lives. God knows how many months we will live, and we are not given a minute longer, Job 14:5. Are you telling me this is not the case?

Dee: No, I am not. But I am telling you that many people die because of the choices that they or others make. That is it. God gives us choices to live our lives; unfortunately other person's choices impact our sense of safety, protection, security, shame, and hope.

Allyson: Well, I can appreciate and understand that, for sure.

Staying Connected

Allyson: One of my favorite quotes by Rumi is that we are all just walking each other home. But we are walking on different paths that lead to this place or experience. Throughout this book, we have stressed the importance of connection, the fact that we are social beings and we need to be connected to a bigger purpose, a body of like-minded people, and a process that gives us direction and affirmation while walking on the healing path. My hope and prayer is that these stories connect us to embracing the Great Mystery, and to acknowledging that we have a choice, we are ultimately made of the stars.

Dee: It's about our Creator, the spiritual side of us. I mean I know what comforts me, but that doesn't mean what I say will convince somebody else. I only have evidence of what I can share in stories. But there is that Great Mystery that exists out there. Do we want to call on it or not?

Allyson: Yeah, well I think that's an important part to acknowledge on the healing path, even in this meeting and this book. It is part of the Great Mystery. Five years ago I was talking to you and writing down notes on a hotel notepad about the healing path. I had no idea that we would be writing this today. Somebody said, "How are you going to write this book and manage everything else happening right now?" I said, "Well, the helpers come". They said, "Well, I wish I had some helpers." We all have spiritual helpers that are available to us. I know they are available to me, and I call upon them. This helps me move forward on the healing path. When I forget the helpers are with me, I take the wrong path, I think of unhealthy thoughts, and forget what I believe. This is the secret of the healing path, total awareness of where we are at, who is available to help us, and recognition that we are all star people.

Enduring Well Prayers

This has been a journey. We are grateful. We started talking about this book more than two years ago. We had many thoughts about the book, the process, how to write it, what to include, whom to include, and even publishing. We felt inadequate and vulnerable at times. We realize there is so much that is missing from this book and so many other clinical and practical applications to include if we had more time. But we do not have more time. Our prayer is that these stories, conversations, theories research, and ideas will help you walk on a healing path. Know that you are not alone on the path. We begin each day seeking connection, the end of suffering, seeking truth, love, and understanding about our sacred place in the world. You are sacred. The path is wide open and welcomes everyone in.

Practice on the Healing Path

Reflect on your own spirituality, forgiveness, and gratitude using these scales.

The Service-user Recovery Evaluation scale (SeRvE) scale is used in recovery and clinical settings to document spirituality. It includes 9 questions about personal religious beliefs and practices. Consider your responses to these questions, and note that God could be replaced by a higher power, divine spirit, or force for good (Barber et al., 2012)

- I feel I am loved by God
- My faith and spiritual belief is helpful to me
- I find it helpful to pray
- I feel spiritual power and forces are controlling me or others
- I feel that God has a purpose for my life.

The Heartland Forgiveness scale has been used to assess forgiveness and includes 18 questions. Consider how you might respond to these sample questions.

- I continue to be hard on others who have hurt me.
- I don't stop criticizing myself for negative things I've felt, thought, said, or done.
- If others mistreat me, I continue to think badly of them.
- It's really hard for me to accept negative situations that aren't anybody's fault.

For more on the HFS see the resources section.

The Gratitude Questionnaire is one example of how clinicians assess gratitude, with responses based on a 7-point scale of strongly disagree to strongly agree. Consider how you might answer these sample questions.

- I have so much in life to be thankful for.
- If I had to list everything that I felt grateful for, it would be a very long list.
- I am grateful to a wide variety of people.
- As I get older I find myself more able to appreciate the people, events, and situations that have been part of my life.

For more on the Gratitude Questionnaire, see the resources section.

Resources

Heartland Forgiveness Scale, https://www.heartlandforgiveness.com/

SeRve Scale by Barber and Colleagues, Cambridge University Press, https://www.cambridge.org/core/journals/the-psychiatrist/article/importance-of-spiritual-wellbeing-in-assessment-of-recovery-the-serviceuser-recovery-evaluation-serve-scale/5B4CBF49C856346435A8128873C92C13

The Gratitude Questionnaire-6 (GQ-6), https://ppc.sas.upenn.edu/resources/questionnaires-researchers/gratitude-questionnaire

References

Barber, J. M., Parkes, M., Parsons, H., & Cook, C. C. H. (2012). Importance of spiritual well-being in assessment of recovery: The Service-user Recovery Evaluation (SeRvE) scale. *The Psychiatrist, 36*(12), 444–450. 10.1192/pb.bp.111.037838

Breen, W. E., Kashdan, T. B., Lenser, M. L., & Fincham, F. D. (2010). Gratitude and forgiveness: Convergence and divergence on self-report and informant ratings. *Personality and Individual Differences, 49*(8), 932–937. 10.1016/j.paid.2010.07.033

Felitti, V. J., Anda, R. F., Nordenberg, D., Williamson, D. F., Spitz, A. M., Edwards, V., Koss, M. P., & Marks, J. S. (1998). Relationship of childhood abuse and household dysfunction to many of the leading causes of death in adults. The Adverse Childhood Experiences (ACE) Study. *American Journal of Preventive Medicine, 14*(4), 245–258. 10.1016/s0749-3797(98)00017-8

Gaventa, W. (2013). Forgiveness, gratitude, and spirituality. In M. L. Wehmeyer (Ed.), *The Oxford handbook of positive psychology and disability* (p. 0). Oxford University Press. 10.1093/oxfordhb/9780195398786.013.013.0016

Helming, M. B. (2011). Healing through prayer: A qualitative study. *Holistic Nursing Practice, 25*(1), 33–44. 10.1097/HNP.0b013e3181fe2697

Rohr, R. (2021). *Breathing under water.* Franciscan Media. Cincinnati, OH.

Thompson, L. Y., Snyder, C. R., Hoffman, L., Michael, S. T., Rasmussen, H. N., Billings, L. S., Heinze, L., Neufeld, J. E., Shorey, H. S., Roberts, J. C., & Roberts, D. E. (2005). Dispositional forgiveness of self, others, and situations. *Journal of Personality, 73*(2), 313–359. 10.1111/j.1467-6494.2005.00311.x

Index